UNFAILING FAITH

LESSONS FROM MY CANCER JOURNEY

Praise for Unfailing Faith

Unfailing Faith is not mere theory—it is the product of wrestling with truth in the brutal face of the reality of death. It is a lived faith. A faith that brought assurance and peace. No matter what was happening to his body, Wolfi chose to believe God in the mystery, remaining confident in God's love and presence because of the certainties of faith. Knowing and living these truths is a game-changer in not losing hope in great adversity.

This journey was not for the faint-hearted. I had a front row seat and I saw the struggle when the circumstances did not make sense—and then the peace and surrender that came from his absolute trust in God. He believed these truths until his last breath. No resignation, daring to trust God until the very end. My hero of faith.

I am beyond thankful for his efforts to write this book, giving me an anchor in my faith as I try to make sense of my incalculable loss.

ALI ECKLEBEN
Married to Wolfgang Eckleben for 33 years
Co-founder and pastor of Every Nation London

On September 13, 2024, my good friend and ministry colleague, Wolfi Eckleben, passed from this life into eternity. While cancer violently attacked his body, Wolfi spent the last few months of his life writing *Unfailing Faith*. With an open and vulnerable heart, Wolfi shared both the struggle and the victory he experienced as he grappled with the reality of a terminal cancer diagnosis. He approached the end of his race the same way he approached his life—with a "persuaded and confident faith" in his Lord and Savior, Jesus Christ. Wolfi remained convinced that nothing in life or death would separate him from the love of God. And now he is home. And he is healed. And he is whole. Wolfi's final words are our invitation to a life of faith, hope, and love.

STEVE MURRELL
Co-founder and president, Every Nation Churches & Ministries
Professor, Every Nation Seminary

I first met Wolfi in the late 1990s when he and Ali were leading the thriving church they had planted on a London university campus. Their vibrant faith in Jesus, serious engagement with scripture and culture has been accompanied by years of faithful service. I couldn't put this beautiful memoir down—as I read, I was drawn closer to Jesus and inspired to press on and run my own race. For anyone asking searching questions about suffering and faith, I highly recommend *Unfailing Faith* and I commend the integrity of its author and the Lord he loved and served.

DR AMY ORR-EWING
Author, speaker, theologian

I have had the privilege of walking with Wolfi and Ali for almost 30 years. Their lives have been a testimony to God's faithfulness and to their persistence in faith. Whether it is the great church they planted in London or the dozens of churches they planted throughout Europe, their unwavering faith has always been a powerful testimony in every endeavor, yet the quality of faith they displayed as they faced Wolfi's cancer diagnosis surpassed everything I had seen in their lives. Wolfi, who is in heaven now, lived far longer than the doctors expected; however, this is only half the story. In his sufferings, Wolfi learned to boldly face one of the great conundrums of the Christian faith: why isn't everyone healed, especially those who truly believe? This book, *Unfailing Faith,* is a journey into a place of faith which will never fail.

JIM LAFFOON
International leadership team, Every Nation Churches
International director, Every Nation Schools of Empowerment

I wholeheartedly endorse *Unfailing Faith,* a powerful exploration of faith in the face of life's greatest challenges. Written by Wolfi during his final days battling cancer, this poignant narrative delves into the profound questions surrounding faith in Jesus. Even as Wolfi courageously asks, "What will the trials we face do to the faith we have in Jesus?", he invites the reader to reflect on and examine their own faith journey. From beginning to end, his life embodies the unshakable faith he describes. His final chapter offers hope and insights into life beyond the grave for those who follow Jesus. *Unfailing Faith* is a must-read for anyone seeking inspiration and strength for their faith in the midst of life's challenges.

KEVIN YORK
Vice president, Every Nation Churches & Ministries

Are you facing a personal crisis or suffering? Do you have questions about the tension between your faith and the extreme suffering you see in the world? Are you struggling with doubt or disappointment in your spiritual journey? Do you long for a deeper, more resilient faith?

My dear friend Wolfi deeply wrestles with these questions, making complex spiritual truths accessible — bringing gentle encouragement as well as challenging and profound truths that invite the reader to develop a faith that remains unshaken by life's inevitable storms.

ROGER PEARCE
Regional leader, Every Nation Southern Africa

Tammy and I first met Wolfi when we joined Every Nation London ten years ago, and as we grew in friendship and ministry, we have seen his life and leadership up close — especially in the details of ministry succession planning in the past couple of years. We can say with confidence that integrity defined his character. Many of his best leadership moments began with "I was REAPing my Bible this morning and..." because he was the same person privately and publicly, who had a living relationship with Jesus, from which he loved well and led. You will feel his love for people (including you!) and passion for the gospel in this book. Wolfi laboured tirelessly to lay a good foundation in many lives and in our church, passing on his "ways in Christ Jesus" (1 Corinthians 4:17), for which we are eternally thankful. We believe that his faith — gritty, ambitious, hopeful (and sometimes stubborn) faith — will be passed on to you through this book.

DAVID AND TAMMY DANIEL
Lead pastors, Every Nation London

Two friends and I were standing at Wolfi's bedside, just days after he'd had a debilitating seizure. As we were about to leave, he quietly said, *"I just don't want anyone's faith to fail because of what I'm going through."* We prayed with him to see that desire fulfilled. This book you are holding is more than words on paper. It is an urgent appeal, from a faith-filled heart, despite contrary circumstances, to hold onto what is more precious than gold — an unfailing faith. I found my heart renewed with faith and hope as I weighed up Wolfi's exhortations and practical guidelines to grasp and live the title of this book. It is something Wolfi modelled right to the end.

FRANS OLIVIER
European director of evangelism, Every Nation

In his typically provocative, honest and humorous style—traits that I admired in the man I knew as a friend and served alongside for 25 years—Wolfi lays out the truths about faith that anchored his own life, and that he lived and taught so compellingly. *Unfailing Faith* provokes me to a life of faith and to live for God's purposes. I recommend this book to anyone, especially those needing hope and encouragement in the face of life's many painful and unpredictable trials.

ANDREW HOLMES
Pastor, Every Nation London

Every Christian needs to read and wrestle with the truths shared in this book. For the storms of life will come, and when they do, we will need faith that is unfailing! This book teaches us how to build such a faith so that when we get to heaven, we may receive the crown of life that is promised to those who love God. I am forever grateful to Wolfi for modelling unfailing faith throughout the years that I knew him, right up until he left this earthly life. You will be encouraged, blessed and challenged by this book, I highly recommend it.

LIZ LUGT
Pastor at Every Nation London, organisational health consultant

A read as gritty, real, and strong as the writer himself. Chapter after chapter, I could feel a strengthened crystallisation of my personal confessions of faith in the Lord. The words are weighty in the reality of the context they're being written in. In the midst of the greatest pain, testing, and trial, we hear Wolfi cheer us, urge us, shake us up: "Friends, do not lose your faith!" I am more than convinced through the presentation of scripture and the testimony of this hero to pursue this quality of faith. There is helpful application and the inclusion of skillfully poised questions to provoke the development of our faith. This is a bootcamp-style handbook of faith for every believer.

ROMONA MCCRINDLE
Missionary, church planter and lead pastor, Every Nation Glasgow

It's one thing to talk about faith, it's another thing to live it. My dear friend Wolfi is a man who not only spoke words of faith, he lived by faith. In *Unfailing Faith*, Wolfi points us to the God who is our rock, the God who does not change, the God about whom Jesus said, "Have faith in God." Wolfi's hope was not in healing, but in the gospel. Through the good news of who Jesus is and what he did, God gives us confidence in our eternal destiny: to live is Christ, and to die is gain. I highly recommend this book!

TOM JACKSON
Director, Every Nation School of Ministry in Europe
Professor, Every Nation Seminary

Wolfgang Eckleben's life story of developing a fighting faith is practical, real, helpful and inspiring. He and his wife Ali, trusted the Lord for the strength to overcome when medicine had come to the end of its effectiveness, and those who practiced it had nothing hopeful to say. His resilience allowed him to stare down death as he entered into glory!

BRETT FULLER
Senior pastor, Grace Covenant Church in Chantilly, Virginia

Pastor Wolfi has traced for us his own journey of not fearing any evil as the Chief Shepherd has walked with, comforted and protected him through the valley of the shadow of death. His unwavering faith has pleased God, and he will be greatly rewarded.

MANNY CARLOS
Bishop of Victory church in Manila, Philippines
Professor, Every Nation Seminary

UNFAILING FAITH

LESSONS FROM MY CANCER JOURNEY

WOLFGANG ECKLEBEN

EVERY NATION
LONDON

AN EVERY NATION LONDON PUBLICATION

Unfailing Faith: Lessons From My Cancer Journey

First published in 2024
For information contact:
6 Staveley Gardens, London, United Kingdom
www.wolfinlondon.com
www.everynation.london

ISBN Number:
978-1-9999804-7-4 Paperback
978-1-9999804-8-1 eBook

Cover design: Amy Eckleben

To all who have prayed and believed with Ali and I
on this cancer journey.

Then many will give thanks on our behalf for the gift that came to us through the prayers of many.

— 2 CORINTHIANS 1:10-11 CSV —

Contents

Foreword ... *1*

Editor's Note ... *3*

INTRODUCTION
Why this book ... *5*

CHAPTER ONE
You have cancer ... *11*

CHAPTER TWO
What can separate you? ... *17*

CHAPTER THREE
Resurrection faith ... *25*

CHAPTER FOUR
Who gave me this cancer? ... *35*

CHAPTER FIVE
When faith fails ... *45*

CHAPTER SIX
No! ... *51*

CHAPTER SEVEN
Being more than a conqueror ... *55*

CHAPTER EIGHT
Becoming fully persuaded ... *59*

CHAPTER NINE
The mysteries and the certainties of faith ... *67*

CHAPTER TEN
Being persuaded about death and eternity ... *73*

CHAPTER ELEVEN
Being persuaded about God's unchanging love and goodness ... *81*

CHAPTER TWELVE
Being persuaded about the resurrected Lord Jesus Christ ... *89*

CHAPTER THIRTEEN
To live is Christ ... *97*

CHAPTER FOURTEEN
To die is gain ... *109*

TOOLKIT
How to grow your faith through REAPing the Bible ... *117*

Acknowledgements ... *121*

About the author ... *123*

Further resources ... *124*

Foreword

I had known Wolfgang Eckleben, Wolfi from this point on, for over a decade but my two-year journey with him in an intense friendship began where this book begins. I had called Wolfi for something I can't even recall right now. When he answered, he told me he was on the way to the hospital because a nagging pain in his back had become unbearable. I was concerned so later I called back to see what the results were and heard the shocking news that he was diagnosed with cancer and was on his way home to talk with his family. At that point I heard the Lord say, "You will be this man's friend for this entire journey."

In this book you will learn things about Wolfi that I learned in the rich exchange of friendship. Things that only a "fiery trial" can reveal after the dross has been burned away. He was a man of deep faith. He had an unrelenting drive to build the church and reach the nations. He loved people and he was passionate about the truth. But Wolfi would be the first to tell you this was not intended to be a book about him. It is a book for people and especially a certain kind of people.

Unfailing Faith needs to be read by every person that has found themselves in places of ongoing suffering. It needs to be read by the person that is consumed with an overpowering question: Why? Why is God silent right now? Why doesn't God do something to change this? Why are the promises seemingly unfulfilled? Why me?

Unfailing Faith needs to be read by every person asking the next question: How? How do I move forward in faith, believing with this situation unresolved? Can I believe for anything? How do I view God in this "allowed trial"? How is God viewing me right now?

When Wolfi began this book, he was not even sure he would be able to finish it. When I asked him why he was writing it, his answer was: "I want to make sure that my situation is properly understood in light of scripture and that no one loses one ounce of their faith in God and his promises because of it, especially if this ends in me standing in front of Jesus very soon."

Wolfi was keenly aware of testimonies of people that had left the faith because in their minds God didn't do what he said he would do. This book is a prevention from that kind of thinking. It is an antidote for unbelief when the "mysteries of sovereignty" come to bear on our personal circumstances. It is a defence to keep the enemy of our soul at bay when life takes a bad turn and seems to be unchanging.

It is important to say this book is filled with the living presence of Jesus. Bolstered by scripture, this book exalts the fact that we are all headed to a glorious eternity.

You will gain strength from the words in these chapters that will sustain you in your battle. You will be inspired and blessed as you read.

Finally, it is Wolfi in print. He was a man for Jesus, a man of great faith, a man of love for the people he served and a truly great friend. He was a man of UNFAILING FAITH. I miss him.

RUSS AUSTIN
Founding pastor of South Point Community Church
Jacksonville, Florida

Editor's Note

I am writing this, with tears, on September 13, 2024. This morning, Wolfi died.

In the pain and in the questions that remain, this book has answers. It started out as a sermon, which Wolfi preached after two and a half years of cancer on April 14, 2024. Frail yet strong, he stepped onto the stage of Every Nation London that day, the church he and Ali planted 30 years prior. His message was entitled, *How to have a faith that does not fail.*

That would be his last sermon. In the days afterwards, Wolfi felt God impress on him to turn that message into a book. He had been writing another book, working title *Carry Your Cheese*, but he paused that and spent much of what would be his remaining months on the book you are now reading.

On the cover is a photograph of Wolfi running as a young athlete, aged about 17, around the time he chose to follow Jesus. Alongside is 2 Timothy 4:7-8 in Wolfi's own handwriting. His family found this scripture in his journal, where he had recorded it in his final months. These are moments from the start of his race, and from its end.

Unfailing Faith is the last public message of a man who had, as that verse says, run the race and kept the faith. A man whose faith in Jesus, the Lord and the Christ, did not fail—even in the face of death. A man who prayed in his last days that your faith would not fail, neither in the face of his death nor in the face of anything you are up against.

MARTINA LEES
London, United Kingdom

INTRODUCTION

Why this book

In this world you will have trouble.
But take heart! I have overcome the world[1]
- JESUS -

I am starting to write this book in April 2024, shortly after receiving the unexpected grim prognosis by my oncologist here in London that I have stage 4 melanoma cancer. The prediction is that I probably only have three short months to live, if not just a few short weeks.

Cancer is not the first serious physical trial that has severely tested my faith. I became a committed follower of Jesus in my final year of school while at the height of a thriving national athletics career in South Africa. At the same time my body was shutting down with a mysterious type of arthritis, but there was no solution to the medical trial I was facing. For the next almost 40 years, crippling pain was part of my daily struggle until a medical solution was eventually found. Now, these many years later, I have this terminal cancer diagnosis.

Forty is the number of testing in the Bible, and perhaps, like me, you are facing a similarly challenging time right now.

Jesus was definitely right when he said "*in this world you will have trouble*", or, as another translation puts it, "*many trials and*

1 John 16:33 NIV

sorrows"[2]. But how do we *take heart* and experience the *overcoming* that he promised in our trials and sorrow?

Please understand that there is a lot at stake. Every test and trial is a fight for your faith. It is a fight in which you must answer the bigger questions: can I really trust God? Is he faithful and able to do what he has promised?

The ultimate question is: what will the trials we face do to the faith we profess to have in Jesus Christ?

This book aims to strengthen your faith so that it will not fail in even the most adverse of circumstances or trouble. I want to show you that having an unfailing faith is possible by building your persuasions on what I will call *the certainties of faith*, rather than *the mysteries of faith.*

Right now, as I face this cancer challenge, I do have great faith for my healing, but we must be honest and acknowledge that there is also much *mystery* about healing, with some being healed and others not, and some prayers being answered, while others are not.

As I sought the Lord's wisdom to face this tension on my cancer journey, it became clear to me that a faith that does not fail cannot be dependent on whether I am physically healed or not. Instead, it must be securely established on the absolute certainties of the gospel, of which every believer can be fully persuaded.

I write this book to support these faith convictions, with the hope that it will help you strengthen and grow a persuaded, confident faith that does not fail under the pressure of *any* circumstances you may face in this life.

The apostle Paul declared that he had a *"persuaded"* (NKJV) or a *"convinced"* (NIV) faith:

> *For I am convinced that neither death nor life, neither angels nor demons, neither the present nor the future, nor any powers, neither height nor depth nor anything else in all creation, will*

2 John 16:33 NLT

be able to separate us from the love of God that is in Christ Jesus our Lord.[3]

He had a faith by which he was fully persuaded that *nothing* — neither death nor life nor any other thing — would be able to separate him from the love of God.

Nothing! This is certainly a bold statement when you consider the severe trials Paul faced, including:

Hard labour
Imprisoned
Whipped
Faced death again and again
Once stoned, then left for dead
Shipwrecked three times
Adrift at sea a whole night and day
Faced danger from rivers and robbers
Faced danger from his own people, the Jews, as well as from the Gentiles. And from those who claimed to be believers but were not
Faced danger in the cities, the deserts, and on the seas
Worked hard and long, with many sleepless nights
Have been hungry and thirsty, often going without food
Shivered in the cold, without enough clothing to keep him warm
Carried the daily weight of his calling and concern for all the churches[4]

Wow, talk about facing *"trouble and sorrows in this world"*!

Yet in all of this, Paul says he has found a faith by which *nothing* — not one of the things listed above, nor death itself — would be able to separate the believer from God. What kind of extraordinary faith is this?

3 Romans 8:38-39 NIV
4 2 Corinthians 11:23-28

This book shares my current reality of cancer threatening to imminently end my life, and explains the faith posture my wife, Ali, and I are taking in response to this.

I want to show you how you can have and grow such a resilient, confident, persuaded faith that is unfailing and unchanged by circumstances you face. A faith built on the absolute certainties of the gospel of Jesus Christ, while at the same time empowering you to believe God boldly in the mysteries as well.

Beyond the information in the book, this kind of faith is received both as a gift of faith and as a spirit of faith, which I am praying will be imparted to you as you read this book. So please open your heart wide and be ready to have your faith strengthened in preparation for what awaits you. God has a good plan[5] for your life and future, no matter how you feel about it right now.

From my experience, the start of anyone stepping into God's calling starts with a simple, *"Here I am, Lord, use me for your glory."* Try stopping for some moments today and saying that to him, and see what he will set in motion to launch you into his good purpose for your life.

My faith before cancer

Faith, of course, is not just for overcoming trouble. It is firstly about being united with God by his amazing grace and for living to pursue and fulfil his great call on our lives. That all involves faith, and what I will share with you has been forged in my personal life of following Jesus since young adulthood.

Having grown up in South Africa, Ali and I both became committed followers of Jesus after completing our school years. Shortly after getting married a few years later, we heard a call from God to plant a new church that reaches the nations and campuses of Europe from the heart of London.

This was over 30 years ago. In 1993, we arrived with our two backpacks and a vision in what we like to call the greatest city in

5 Jeremiah 29:11

the world. On this journey, we have experienced his promises fulfilled over and over again in incredible ways. The Lord has opened doors to the nations, and leaders have been raised and sent out to start more churches across Europe and beyond. Thousands of lives have been changed. God has consistently provided abundantly for the mission he gave us. Relationships and marriages have been healed and transformed. I could go on and on. All of it has required and shaped the same fully persuaded faith by which we now face this cancer.

Our great hope is not in my healing, but in the confidence of the gospel. I may well no longer be alive when you read this. But no matter what happens and how and when, I want you to know that in this most dire of trials with cancer, Ali and I are experiencing a persuaded faith that has not failed, and I believe will not fail no matter what I will still face.

I commit to doing my very best to communicate and impart to you the revelation, gift and spirit of faith that will give you all you need to have *a faith that does not fail* in whatever trial and trouble you may face in life, and to be more than a conqueror[6] in Christ Jesus as you do.

6 Romans 3:31

CHAPTER ONE

You have cancer

They do not fear bad news.
They confidently trust the Lord to care for them[1]
- KING DAVID'S PSALMS -

Nine years ago, Ali noticed an unusual-looking mole on my back. It turned out to be cancerous. This was swiftly cut out, and the good doctor scribbled an encouraging note at the end of the medical report:

> Mr Eckleben,
> the lesion was completely
> excised and should not
> cause you any more problems
>
> End of report Dr

Besides staying committed to a sometimes inconvenient annual dermatology checkup, I did not pay much attention to this close call with cancer.

But two and a half years ago, while I was doing a leader's weekend with a church in England's beautiful northwest, I began to feel unusual pain in my back. It took three months to diagnose this as

1 Psalm 112:7

stage four melanoma cancer, which by this time had metastasised throughout my back, spine, lung, liver and up towards my head. And yes, I needed to determine that metastasised meant "spread". A cancer diagnosis is also an enrolment in the school of medical terms and procedures.

The prognosis was as little as three months. From there I embarked on a rollercoaster ride of treatments that included immunotherapy, radiotherapy for tumours on my spine, Gamma Knife therapy for tumours on my brain, and an emergency operation on a tumour pressing into my spinal cord. The latter left me using a catheter for a few weeks due to losing control of my bladder and bowels.

It all came with an onslaught of good and bad news. Against expectations, the cancer first responded positively, then advanced again. The immunotherapy was working, then no longer. Cancer blocker pills followed to see if those would work. They did, for a few months. Plus, there was all the medication to manage skeletal and nerve pain and a raft of side effects from the various treatments. The worst of these were loss of appetite, frequent vomiting, weakness, tiredness, extreme weight loss, and generally feeling nauseous most of the time.

With the cancer being as pervasive as it was, there was little expectation that I would pull through. But I did. Quite unexpectedly, I began to feel quite well and started to function normally again, which seemed quite miraculous at that stage. A radiotherapist friend who looked at my scans commented: *"Wolfi, you don't look on the outside like what I know is going on inside of you!"*

However, two years after the original diagnosis, the cancer was spreading again. To give you an insight into how such news can come to a cancer patient, let me describe the day I learnt about the new tumour activity in my brain.

A previous scan had shown that there were about nine small tumours active in my brain. To treat these, I was scheduled for a session of Gamma Knife radiosurgery, in which very precise radiation beams destroy small to medium sized brain tumours. I was familiar with this quite scary procedure as I'd had the same a year previously. It involved screwing a carbon fibre frame straight into my skull bone, using four screws under local anaesthetic alone. On the upside, this treatment was done in the private Cromwell Hospital, which has the best hospital food menu I have ever had!

Once the frame is attached to the skull, you are taken for a pre-op scan, which is used to plan the exact radiosurgery involved. The next step should be the actual treatment, and soon, you should be able to have that delicious private hospital lunch and be discharged. That's what happened to me the first time, and as a bonus, I had not even had any adverse side effects.

This time, however, after the pre-op scans, two medical staff came into the room. I could see by their sober demeanour that something was very wrong. And it was.

Now there were 40

We'd been quite light-hearted and cheerful in our interactions throughout the morning, as a dose of humour seems to help in these settings. But humour could not hide the reality: the scan showed that there were not just nine tumours, as expected from the previous scan. Now they had found over forty.

This was beyond the scope of what the Gamma Knife therapy was able to treat. The frame was unceremoniously screwed off my skull, and I was discharged.

No more options

The following week, we sat in my oncologist's office considering whether there were any further treatment options available to stop this ever-increasing spread of cancer through my body. The conclusion was that all viable treatment options had been exhausted. I would be discharged to "best end of life care", with a life expectancy of three months, perhaps only a few short weeks.

As we left the office, we stated again that we were people of faith and were trusting our God fully with what lay ahead. That's how we left the hospital to face my future in April 2024.

How to face bad news by faith

A few years previously, a good friend who had a high-powered banking career in the City of London was unexpectedly made redundant and accompanied out of the fancy office building into unemployment street. They had just bought a new house. It was not a good time to be made redundant.

He was well qualified with an excellent resume and experience, yet inexplicably he could not secure a new job for nearly two years. This was a severe faith-testing time for him.

However, during the repeated job application refusals and interview rejections, he often confessed a wonderful promise from the Psalms that sustained him through this challenging season: *"They do not fear bad news; they confidently trust the Lord to care for them."* It continues in the following verse: *"Their hearts are secure, they will have no fear; in the end, they will look in triumph on their foes."*[2]

The "they" here is not just anyone. It refers to "the righteous", meaning those who have, by faith, put their trust in God. For the New Testament believer, that would translate as follows:

> *Those who have put their faith in the Lord Jesus Christ will not fear bad news. They will confidently trust the Lord to care for them. They will have no fear. They will trust that in the end they will be victorious over their enemy and troubles in this world.*

This promise has also been my confession and anchor since I initially received the bad news that I had cancer: *"I will not fear bad news. My heart is steadfast, trusting fully in my Lord."*

2 Psalm 112:7—8 NIV

I don't deny the reality of cancer and all that could happen, but I do face these brutal cancer facts with confident faith that declares:

> I will fear no bad news.
> I will confidently trust in the Lord.
> I will not fear.
> I trust that in the end, I will be victorious.
> In the end (whatever that looks like), I will overcome through Jesus my Lord.
> I will be more than a conqueror in Christ Jesus my Lord.

I have cancer, but God...

CHAPTER TWO

What can separate you?

Can anything ever separate us from Christ's love?[1]

- THE APOSTLE PAUL -

I don't deny the reality of cancer and all that could happen according to the medical prognosis. I am fully aware that, without a true miraculous intervention, I will not be alive by the time you read this. In fact, I would argue that just being here now and able to write, over two years after being told I have three months to live, is already a miracle. But I do face these brutal facts with confident faith in the Lord Jesus Christ. I believe that he can heal me, and that is what I am holding out for.

I am also fully convinced and aware that I have an enemy, the devil, whose plan is always to kill, steal and destroy.[2]

Please don't get distracted by my reference to the devil, Satan, or evil here. The Bible clearly teaches that we have such an enemy, and we must be alert to his evil schemes. Knowing your enemy's plan and objective is a real advantage in any battle, so let's be clear: the enemy's strategy is always to separate you from God in whatever way he can.

1 Romans 8:35

2 John 10:10

Satan separates, God unites

To *separate* is the one word that best describes Satan's mission against humanity, and it most accurately describes what sin does. He started in the Garden of Eden where he succeeded in turning Adam and Eve away from God, driving a wedge of distrust and sin between them and their Creator. Sin is the ultimate separator between God and man, and with it sin separates you from God's peace, purpose, hope, health, your relationships, and everything good that Satan can get his hands on.

> *If Satan cannot separate you through sin, he will do all he can to separate you through trials and circumstances.*

God's mission, on the other hand, is to restore relationship with you, having made the Way for all to come to him[3] through believing the gospel of the Lord Jesus Christ.

Paul shows that there is much at stake when he calls this *"the good fight for the true faith"*, through which you *"hold tightly to the eternal life to which God has called you"*.[4] There is no greater prize to fight for in this life than this. I like to say that *the prize you are fighting for will determine how you fight.*

It is in the light of this battle that Paul poses the crucial faith question to us:

> *Can anything ever separate us from Christ's love?*

He continues:

> *Does it mean he no longer loves us if we have trouble or calamity, or are persecuted, or hungry, or destitute, or in danger, or threatened with death?*[5]

He is asking a big question of those who say that we are believers in the gospel of Jesus Christ, and who have confessed him as Lord

3 John 15:6
4 1 Timothy 6:12
5 Romans 8:35

of our lives: if you truly believe these great benefits and blessings of the gospel, are there any circumstances in this life that could cause you to doubt that God loves you? Is there anything that could cause your faith to fail?

Will you give up your faith when you face some trouble? Or when you are persecuted or resisted? Or when you are hungry? When you lose your job and can't pay the bills? Or because you are lonely, will you compromise what you believe? Or because God is not answering your prayer like you asked? Or you come across something in the Bible that you don't understand? Perhaps you would overcome all that, but what if things become life-threatening: will you still hold on to your faith?

What circumstances have the power to separate you from the love of God? Is there anything valuable enough to give up your faith for?

Seeing the bigger picture through Romans 8

An eternal perspective is a very empowering lens through which to evaluate what you are facing in life. If you are not familiar with the gospel and are looking for a summary of this great message, you will find no more profound text than the statements, truths and claims made by Paul in Romans chapter eight to help you understand the Christian faith. Here you find what I like to call the great summary of the benefits and blessings for everyone who believes the gospel of Jesus Christ and follows him as Lord and Saviour.

Consider the following two examples of how Paul presents the eternal perspectives we can have on the temporary trials and sorrows we face in this life:

> *Yet what we suffer now is nothing compared to the glory he will reveal to us later.*[6]
>
> *So we don't look at the troubles we can see now; rather, we fix our gaze on things that cannot be seen. For the things we*

6 Romans 8:18

see now will soon be gone, but the things we cannot see will last forever.[7]

This perspective empowers us, the believers, to lift up our eyes above the troubles we experience now—knowing that they will not last forever and will soon pass away—and choosing to rather fix our gaze on things that cannot be seen now but that will last forever.

Experience the present blessings

We also do not just look away from present troubles and trials with dogged discipline, but very much *look past them* with great joy to the blessings and benefits which are for us to experience in Christ *now*. These are as real as our present trials, and make up the full experience of life in Christ that we have in this present life. Consider the following in Romans 8 as reminders of the incredible blessings available to you as a believer every day. Are these part of the lens through which you see your trials?

Verse 1-2: God has forgiven our sins and we are free!

*So now there is **no** condemnation for those who belong to Christ Jesus. And because you belong to him, the power of the life-giving Spirit has **freed** you from the power of sin that leads to death.*

Verse 11: God lives in us! And we have eternal life!

*The Spirit of God, who raised Jesus from the dead, lives **in** you. And just as God raised Christ Jesus from the dead, he will give **life** to your mortal bodies by this same Spirit living within you.*

Verse 15-16: We are children of God!

*So you have not received a spirit that makes you fearful slaves. Instead, you received God's Spirit when he adopted you as **his** own children. Now we call him, "Abba, Father."*

7 2 Corinthians 4:18

Verse 26-27: The Holy Spirit is our Helper!

And the Holy Spirit helps us in our weakness. For example, we don't know what God wants us to pray for. But the Holy Spirit prays ***for*** *us with groanings that cannot be expressed in words. And the Father who knows all hearts knows what the Spirit is saying, for the Spirit pleads for us believers in harmony with God's own will.*

Verse 28: God is at work for our good in all things!

And we know that God causes everything to work together for the ***good*** *of those who love God and are called according to his purpose for them.*

Verse 31: God is for us, not against us!

What shall we say about such wonderful things as these? If ***God*** *is for us, who can ever be against us?*

Verse 32: God is our generous giving Father!

Since he did ***not*** *spare even his own Son but gave him up for us all, won't he also give us everything else?*

Do those incredible blessings not give a wonderful perspective on our temporary trials? And the best is that we receive these by faith through amazing grace, which means they are unearned and undeserved, given freely by God to all who accept the gift of eternal life through faith in Christ Jesus.

The big faith question

And then, right in the heart of this great summary of the blessings and benefits of the gospel, Paul poses his crucial faith question for us:

> *Can anything ever separate us from Christ's love? Does it mean he no longer loves us if we have trouble or calamity, or are*

> *persecuted, or hungry, or destitute, or in danger, or threatened with death?*

No, trouble does not mean that he doesn't love us. But it is an important question to process, because there is much at stake if you don't.

The question is very relevant to me personally as I write this: will I still hold on by faith even in the face of this cancer onslaught?

Will our faith fail in the face of our tragedy, challenges, trials, or death?

Let no one separate

A *faith that will not fail* is one that overcomes all that threatens to *separate* us from God. This is the same covenant word Jesus used when teaching that *no one should separate from* a marriage that has been joined together by God.[8]

It takes us back to the reality that, while Satan's mission is always to separate, God is always in the uniting business. Therefore, let no one and nothing separate anyone from the love of God in Christ. God is for you, and not against you, and he offers you and everyone who calls on his name every help to remain united in covenant relationship with him.

It sadly is true that many will allow trials and sorrows in this life to bring them into unbelief, to separate them from the love of God.

But the good news is that our faith does not need to fail. We *can* be more than conquerors in Christ and can end our race like Paul did, boldly declaring as he crosses the line from this life to the next:

> *I have fought the good fight, I have finished the race, I have kept the faith. Now there is in store for me the crown of righteousness.*[9]

8 Matthew 19:6 NIV

9 2 Timothy 4:7-8 NIV

This is the great prize of having a faith that does not fail. This is the prize that we are fighting for, and that will determine how we fight to hold on to eternal life.

PAUSE TO THINK AND TALK ABOUT IT

⇒ What is the one thing that you found most relevant or helpful in this chapter?

⇒ Pause and make it personal. In the introduction, I shared my cancer diagnosis and prognosis with you. This is my faith challenge. What have you faced? What are you facing? How is your faith doing?

CHAPTER THREE

Resurrection faith

Lord, increase our faith[1]

- THE DISCIPLES -

Faith is not a static thing that you either have or do not have.

In my many years of following Jesus and trying to help others know and follow him, it's become clear to me that not all faith is equal. I've come across weak faith, shallow faith, good-times faith, convenient faith, intellectual faith, emotional faith, foolish faith, presumptuous faith, unfounded faith and misplaced faith. I've also seen strong, growing, consistent and persuaded faith that does not fail.

For Ali and I, our faith has been and is being severely tested through this cancer. Any aspects of shallow, intellectual, or emotional faith we may have had were quickly swept away by the tide of my diagnosis. We have had to dig down deep to reach the proper foundations of our faith. That's what a storm does. I love how The Message translation puts this in James 1:3:

> *You know that under pressure, your faith-life is forced into the open and shows its true colours.*

1 Luke 17:5

I find it helpful to be as clear as possible about what I mean by the definitions and statements that I use, and the following set of statements are the clearest I can come up with to communicate what I mean by *a persuaded faith that will not fail, even under the most severe of troubles:*

Faith is trusting God

I start by understanding that *faith is trusting God.* This focuses my faith exclusively on God, the One in whom I am placing my faith. I don't have faith in faith (especially not my own faith!). My faith is not defined by just being a Christian and calling myself that through habit; nor in the idea that if I believe hard enough, the breakthrough will come.

No, my faith is in God himself, personally, daily, continually. I trust God alone. He is the object of my faith.

Faith is *fully* trusting God

I add the word *fully* to strengthen this definition: *faith is fully trusting God.* The picture I have here is of leaning my whole weight onto an object, and if that object were to collapse or move, I would fall to the ground. I am now *fully trusting* the object of my faith: God.

Faith is fully trusting God's *greatness, wisdom and goodness*

To fully trust God requires being fully convinced that he is fully trust***worthy***. This is only possible if we are confident of the perfect nature and character of the God we say we believe in.

When I created the Follow Course as an intentional discipleship journey to help people know God and grow in their faith, I concluded that every discipleship journey must start with knowing God. To establish this truth, I crafted the statement:

> *What you know and believe about someone will determine how you relate to them.*

This is true, isn't it? And it's the same for having faith in God: *what you know and believe about God will determine how you will trust him.*

This may be an excellent place to pause and ask yourself: what do I believe God is like? Perhaps take some time to write down a few words or sentences that describe what you believe about God's nature and character.

Of course, if what we believe is not shaped by the right sources, our faith will be misguided and will ultimately fail. As Christians, our two primary sources for knowing what God is really like are what he has revealed about himself through the scriptures and through Jesus. From these sources, I conclude the three most important things to believe about God is that: God is *infinitely great*[2], *perfectly wise*[3] and *altogether good*[4]. Or said another way: *faith is fully trusting God's greatness, wisdom and goodness.* Let's consider each of these aspects now.

1 Trusting God's *infinite greatness* means believing that God is almighty and thus able to do all things. He is fully able to do what he promised in his Word. In my case, God *can* heal cancer. God *can* do miracles. God *can* provide for you, whatever your need or circumstance. He *can* forgive sin. He *can* restore that relationship. God *can* deliver you from evil. Paul writes to the disciples under tremendous pressure in the pagan worshipping city of Ephesus: *"God is able to do immeasurably more than all we ask or imagine."*[5] A persuaded faith believes that God is able.

2 Trusting God's *perfect wisdom* means believing that God is all-knowing, eternal and ever-present. Therefore, while I only see a small part of the picture, he always sees the whole. Wisdom includes the timing of things, their fitting together and the process

2 Psalm 96:4, Psalm 145:3
3 Isaiah 28:29, Romans 11:33
4 Exodus 34:6, Psalm 34:8
5 Ephesians 3:20 NIV

of things. It also includes that God always knows and works out the greater purpose of things. I don't understand why I have cancer, nor what its greater purpose may include, but trusting God's wisdom is to submit to the fact that though I don't understand a situation, God always does and is working all things out for his glory, the gospel and my good. A persuaded faith fully trusts God to work according to his wisdom, not mine.

3 Trusting God's ***altogether goodness*** means believing that God is love and always works all things together for the good of those who love him.[6] It means believing that God is always for you, not against you.[7] God's goodness is demonstrated by his presence, so I am comforted and strengthened that even in the valley of the shadow of death, he is with me.[8] God's love for the world was his motivation for the gospel,[9] and his love continues to manifest through his amazing grace to save all who will believe. A persuaded faith believes that God is always and altogether good in every situation.

Of course it is easy to say these statements, but are we still persuaded of these in response to Paul's big question about the trials and sorrows we will face in this world?

This takes us to the next statement to define a fully persuaded faith:

Faith is fully trusting God *in everything at all times*

Not just when all is going well but *in everything at all times*. This is an authentic, fully persuaded faith. No matter the circumstance, I continue to fully trust God that he is great, wise and good at all times and in everything and anything I am going through.

6 Romans 8:28
7 Romans 8:31
8 Psalm 23:4 ESV
9 John 3:16

Next, faith is fully trusting God's *Word*

Because I fully trust God, I can also fully trust what he says. What you believe about someone will determine whether you believe what they say, right?

The same is true with God: what you believe about God will determine whether you believe his Word. You cannot say that you have faith in someone if you do not trust that they will and can do what they say.

Let's take a moment to examine the promises of God on which we build a persuaded, unfailing faith.

The true source of faith

In Romans 10, Paul presents the source of our faith:

> *So faith comes from hearing, that is, hearing the Good News about Christ.*[10]

Note that he says that faith comes "from hearing", and that this "hearing" refers specifically to hearing about the Good News or message about Christ.

Christians often quote this verse as *"faith comes from hearing the word"*, meaning hearing anything in the Bible or one of God's promises. In context, though, this is specifically about hearing the gospel of Jesus Christ: that God so loved us that he gave his only son to die for us, be buried and rise again.

His resurrection from the dead is the Word on which we build our faith. It is the ultimate demonstration of God's greatness, wisdom and goodness. It is how God fulfilled humanity's salvation — just as he had promised and predicted through the prophets of old.

The resurrection must be the foundation of our faith

The resurrection is the foundation on which we can *"fully trust God"* that he will do, and can do, all that he promised throughout the rest of scripture.

10 Romans 10:17

Paul's faith took him to the end of himself. In 2 Corinthians 1:9 he acknowledged that he and his companions *expected to die* because there was no more hope in the natural world. But as a result, he says, they stopped relying on themselves and learned to rely only on God, who raises the dead.

If we believe God raised Jesus from the dead, we can also believe that anything God promises is possible. On the other hand, if we do not believe in the resurrection, we will never have a persuaded faith that fully trusts God. In chapter 12, I will further make the case for having a persuaded faith in the resurrection of Jesus.

Abraham's resurrection faith

Scripture records that Abraham believed the Lord *and was fully convinced that God is able to do whatever he promises.*[11]

What specifically was it that he believed, and what promise was he fully convinced about? It was, in fact, a foreshadowing of the gospel that an only son would miraculously be born into the world, and secondly, that this son would be raised from the dead.

God had promised Abraham that he would have a son as his heir, but there was a big problem. He was way too old. His wife Sarah was both barren and many years past child-bearing age. The promise seemed impossible. As he considered the entire impossibility of ever having the child God had promised him with Sarah, God again reminded him of the promise. In response, Abraham believed the Lord, and miraculously, Isaac was born.

Next, though, there's a great plot twist: God asks Abraham to sacrifice his only son. In obedience, he ends up in that unfathomable moment standing over Isaac on the altar with the knife in his hand. In obedience, he was ready to sacrifice his only son, Isaac, whom he loved.

Abraham must have had a thousand questions, but to those travelling with him, he spoke out the one thing that would make sense of this test God was putting him through: *"Stay here with the*

11 Romans 4:20-21

donkey while I and the boy go over there. We will worship, and then we will come back to you."[12]

Did you read that? ***"Then we will come back to you"***. Abraham believed that he would come back *with Isaac* because he had faith that God could even raise the dead.[13]

This clearly foreshadows the gospel, pointing forward to the death and resurrection of God's own loved son on the cross.

The joy set before Jesus

The apostle John also tries to explain this to the Jewish rulers by telling them that Abraham *"saw it [the coming of Jesus] and was glad"*.[14] The Message version uses even more descriptive language for how Jesus communicated this to the Jews who were struggling to *"see"* this revelation of the resurrection that would change everything through this crucial moment in history: *"Abraham—your 'father'—with elated faith looked down the corridors of history and saw my day coming. He saw it and cheered."*[15]

This was the joy set before Jesus.[16] On the cross, death itself could not separate him from the Father. Through his victory we too can run with endurance the race set before us, empowered to overcome every trial that threatens to separate us from the love of God in Christ Jesus.

Paul summarises Abraham's resurrection faith as follows:

> *Abraham never wavered in believing God's promise. In fact, his faith grew stronger, and in this he brought glory to God.* ***He was fully convinced that God is able to do whatever he promises.***[17]

12 Genesis 22:5 NIV
13 Hebrews 11:19
14 John 8:56
15 John 8:56 The Message
16 Hebrews 12:1-3
17 Romans 4:20-21

This, then, is the final element of what I mean by a persuaded faith that will not fail: it is being fully convinced that God, who raises the dead, is able to do what he has promised.

Summarising fully persuaded faith that does not fail

Let's now tie it together with the series of statements I presented in this chapter, to read through the whole definition again:

> *Faith is fully trusting God—his greatness, wisdom and goodness—in everything at all times, being fully convinced that he is able to do what he has promised.*

PAUSE TO THINK AND TALK ABOUT IT

⇒ What is the one thing that you found most relevant or helpful in this chapter?

⇒ Describe what you have believed about God's nature and character.

⇒ Take some time to think about the definition of a fully persuaded faith that I proposed and consider:

- Do you agree with this definition? What would you add, or remove from it?
- What part of it is most challenging to you?
- What would be helpful to embrace from this definition that would strengthen your faith?

⇒ Do you "see" the revelation of the resurrection faith that Abraham saw?

⇒ How is your faith doing after what you have been or are still going through? How have your circumstances shaped or changed your faith? Would you say it is stronger or weaker? Or still the same?

CHAPTER FOUR

Who gave me this cancer?

Every good and perfect gift is from above,
coming down from the Father[1]
- THE APOSTLE JAMES -

Before we continue considering how to build our faith, we must pause to be transparent about the *sources* of the trials, troubles and tests we face. Where do these come from? Who or what is the cause for giving or allowing cancer to be in my body like this? Why me?

It's important and empowering to know where the tests, trials and troubles you are facing have come from. Being confused or deceived about the source of your troubles will greatly undermine your faith in any battle. Knowing your true enemy is vital to focusing your faith and fighting effectively.

Let's explore what we can learn about this in scripture.

Some trouble is from this world

Jesus made it clear to his disciples that some troubles would be because we are in this fallen world broken by sin and its consequences: "*in this world, you will have trouble*".[2] While God gives common grace to all creation and creatures, we are also all

1 James 1:17 NIV
2 John 16:33 NIV

experiencing the universality of suffering from the effect of sin in this world. In Romans chapter eight, Paul refers to this suffering and how all creation and believers *"groan as in the pains of childbirth"*[3] as we long for a future day of being gloriously freed from all death and decay, released from all sin and suffering. This is our great hope as we struggle with trouble in this world.

Satan's tests, temptation and thorns

The Bible clearly outlines a spiritual realm and a spiritual battle, which manifests in direct attacks against everything good in God's creation.

When Jesus warned Peter that he would be tempted to deny his Lord, he made it clear that this was a test from Satan, not from God, and not just of this world.[4] Later, when Peter wrote his letters to the believers, possibly reflecting on his own experience of when Satan tested him, he warned: *"Your enemy the devil prowls around like a roaring lion looking for someone to devour."*[5]

Paul also wrote that his thorn in the flesh was *"a messenger from Satan"*.[6] We may debate *what* exactly his thorn was, but there is no room for debate about *who* sent it to him. He also instructs the Ephesian believers to *"hold up the shield of faith to stop the fiery arrows of the devil"*.[7]

We wrestle not (just) against flesh and blood (in this world), but against wicked spiritual forces that are set against us with every kind of evil and suffering.[8]

We suffer through our lack of wisdom

We all have a choice to live as the wise or the foolish. Through the Bible, Christians have access to the most incredible treasure trove

3 Romans 8:22
4 Luke 22:31-32
5 1 Peter 5:8 NIV
6 2 Corinthians 12:7
7 Ephesians 6:16
8 Ephesians 6:12 ESV

of wisdom to live well, yet often, we neglect and reject this precious gift and suffer the consequences of our foolishness instead.

Wisdom is the application of knowledge. Knowledge understands that a tomato is a fruit because it meets the botanical definition of a fruit, but wisdom understands that you don't put tomatoes in a fruit salad. In the same way, wisdom can bless, but foolishness can ruin our relationships, finances, health and much more. The book of Proverbs exposes the consequence of foolishness like this: "*People ruin their lives by their own foolishness and then are angry at the Lord.*"[9] Not only does our lack of wisdom destroy our lives, but it also ruins our relationship with God. We don't have to live like this because, "*If you need wisdom, ask our generous God, and he will give it to you. He will not rebuke you for asking.*"[10]

Take a few moments to consider how the following verses may apply to you regarding gaining godly wisdom and rejecting foolishness and its destructive consequences:

> *So be careful how you live. Don't live like fools, but like those who are wise. Make the most of every opportunity in these evil days.*[11]
>
> *For the Lord grants wisdom! From his mouth come knowledge and understanding.*[12]
>
> *Trust in the Lord with all your heart; do not depend on your own understanding. Seek his will in all you do, and he will show you which path to take.*[13]
>
> *All scripture is inspired by God and is useful to teach us what is true and to make us realise what is wrong in our lives. It corrects us when we are wrong and teaches us to do what is*

9 Proverbs 19:3
10 James 1:5
11 Ephesians 5:15-16
12 Proverbs 2:6
13 Proverbs 3:5-6

> *right. God uses it to prepare and equip his people to do every good work.*[14]
>
> *Getting wisdom is the wisest thing you can do! And whatever else you do, develop good judgement.*[15]

To live wisely is to live well, so let's do that!

The consequences of our sin

Much of our suffering and trouble is because of our sinful choices and decisions. We can choose our actions, but we don't get to choose the consequences of our actions. The problem with this is that when it comes to trouble or suffering, you may constantly worry or believe that this is some punishment by God for your sin. That is too heavy a burden for anyone to bear, and the Accuser will do whatever he can to keep you weighed down with guilt, shame and condemnation for as long as he can. So let me briefly remind you about sin and its consequences and how you can cast off that burden.

Believers are *"dead to sin"*,[16] meaning we are no longer slaves to sin, yet we still do sin, and our sinful actions and choices always lead to some measure of death.

> *Temptation comes from our own desires, which entice us and drag us away. These desires give birth to sinful actions. And when sin is allowed to grow, it gives birth to death.*[17]

Sin always separates

The consequence of sin is primarily experienced as *separation*, like Adam and Eve, who were driven out of the Garden and separated from the intimate presence of their Creator. Sin also separates us from our peace, purpose, relationships, hope, blessings and more. The good news is that our Father God is always waiting for us to

14 2 Timothy 3:16-17
15 Proverbs 4:7
16 Romans 6:11 NIV
17 James 1:14-15

come home fully restored. Our part, like the Prodigal Son, is to come to our senses, take full responsibility for whatever the sin was, and turn back home in repentance:

> *Father, I have sinned against both heaven and you, and I am no longer worthy of being called your son.*[18]

You must remember, though, that the enemy is also your Accuser who declares to the Great Judge that you are no longer worthy because of your sin. But in response, God overrules that judgment with the verdict that settles it all:

> *It is finished.*[19]

In other words, it is paid in full! This is how Peter preached this promise after Pentecost:

> *Now repent of your sins and turn to God, so that your sins may be wiped away. Then times of refreshment will come from the presence of the Lord.*[20]

The result that "*will come*" after repentance is refreshment from the presence of God. Repentance must be followed by believing and receiving the Father's complete forgiveness. In response, you are *justified*, just-as-if-I'd never sinned!

Yes, you may still suffer some consequences of sin, but they are not punishment from God. You are his child whom he loves, and he will continue to work all things together for your good—**even** the consequences of your sin.

So, who sent the cancer?

Is cancer from God, Satan, or this world? Or perhaps it is a consequence of my own unhealthy choices? After all, it is skin cancer, and in my youth I spent far too much time sailing and surfing in

18 Luke 15:21
19 John 19:30
20 Acts 3:19-20

the sun and sea without adequate protection. So yes, we can debate the latter three options, but one thing I want to encourage you to be 100% clear about is this:

Cancer and sickness are NOT from God.

Such thinking or theology goes against everything I believe about the nature of the great and good God as he has revealed himself through Jesus the Healer. If his Word reveals his will, his will is clearly for healing and life, not sickness, disease and death. As James declares:

> *Every good and perfect gift is from above, coming down from the Father of the heavenly lights, who does not change like shifting shadows.*[21]

One of the earliest promises the Spirit spoke to me at the start of my cancer journey was from 2 Timothy 4:18:

> *The Lord will deliver me from every evil attack and will bring me safely into his heavenly Kingdom. All glory to God forever and ever! Amen.*

For me, this promise clarified whom this battle was against and what it was about, and it set me up to fight this evil with a faith that does not fail. Here's what I concluded:

- Cancer is from the devil, not from God.
- The enemy's objective is to separate me from the love of God and to doubt his goodness.
- The battle is the kingdom of darkness against the Kingdom of God—and I know who wins!
- Whatever happens, my destiny will *not* be determined by cancer or evil, but my God alone will bring me safely through to his eternal kingdom.
- At stake is God's glory. By the Holy Spirit I will be empowered to have a faith that does not fail, so that God may be glorified

21 James 1:17 NIV

in everything I do and say and believe as I face this trial and suffering.

God does test us

Cancer is from Satan, but God has sovereignly allowed it. God does also test us as we saw in the previous chapter when he asked Abraham to sacrifice his only son Isaac.[22] Abraham passed the test by believing that God would raise his son from the dead, and by his faith, he received righteousness and was promoted to being the father of many nations. Yet God does not test us beyond what we can bear.[23] What's more, God's tests always have a purpose, to see if we are ready for promotion, while Satan's tests are always for your demotion, to break you and separate you.

The opportunity in the trials

Going through trials and troubles is neither easy nor pleasant, but in all these we have a promise: "*we know that God causes everything to work together for good for those who love God and are called according to his purpose for them*".[24] Notice the connection between trials and purpose here. The more confident you are in God and his calling for you, the more empowered you will be to face the trials—not just to survive them but to see God work all things out together for his glory, the gospel, and your good.

As the apostle James reminds us:

> *Dear brothers and sisters, when troubles of any kind come your way, consider it an opportunity for great joy. For you know that when your faith is tested, your endurance has a chance to grow. So let it grow, for when your endurance is fully developed, you will be perfect and complete, needing nothing.*[25]

22 Genesis 22:1-18
23 1 Corinthians 10:13
24 Romans 8:28
25 James 1:2-4

Perfect. Complete. Needing nothing. That's a prize worth fighting for in every trial!

- There is an appointment in every disappointment.
- There is the possibility of a triumph in every trial.
- There is a way to turn your pain into purpose.

In this chapter we looked at the different sources of trials we face in this world. We saw that avoiding being confused or deceived about the source is vital to overcome in this fight for your faith. It's also essential to never forget that God can work all things together for good in every trial, even if you are walking through the shadow of death like I currently am. In all things I pray that nothing will separate you from the love of God and that your faith will not fail!

But next, we must face the fact that, on this journey, sometimes our faith does fail, and how do we handle that?

PAUSE TO THINK AND TALK ABOUT IT

⇒ What is the one thing that you found most relevant or helpful in this chapter?

⇒ What is the most difficult source of trial for you to accept, and why?

⇒ Do you agree that sickness never comes from God? In your own words explain why, or why not?

⇒ Have you ever suffered due to a lack of wisdom? Recall what happened, and what you learnt from this.

CHAPTER FIVE

When faith fails

But I have prayed for you[1]

- JESUS -

Our faith will be tested. And sometimes our faith does fail. Peter's did. Perhaps yours has? Perhaps the trials were just too big and the pain too much to bear, or the cost too high.

If that's where you have found yourself, then this chapter is for you.

In Luke 22, at the end of his last supper with his followers on the eve of his death, Jesus gives Peter a loving warning:

> *Simon, Simon, Satan has asked to sift each of you like wheat. But I have pleaded in prayer for you, Simon, that your faith should not fail. So when you have repented and turned to me again, strengthen your brothers.*[2]

Probably like most of us in such a situation, Peter could not accept that he would ever do such a thing as to deny his Lord. But sadly he did, as he sat warming himself at the fire watching Jesus being mocked, interrogated and beaten — finally exclaiming a third time, *"I don't know the man!"*[3] When he realised what he had done,

1 Luke 22:32 NKJV

2 Luke 22:31-32

3 Matthew 26:74

we read: "*Peter left the courtyard, weeping bitterly.*"[4] His faith had failed. Sin had separated him. Satan had won. Or had he?

This could have been the end of Peter's faith, but did you see what Jesus had said to him at the beginning of this interaction?

But I have prayed for you, that your faith may not fail.

In the same breath as the warning, Jesus spoke hope for Peter's restoration, and a plan for his future. Just like Jeremiah when he prophesied to the exiles in Babylon: "*I know the plans I have for you,*" *says the Lord.* "*They are plans for good and not for disaster, to give you a future and a hope.*"[5]

This is God's heart for you too. The good news is that he is always the God of restoration if we want it. Peter's faith and purpose were restored, and so can yours be — no matter what you have done, how far you have fallen, or what so-called pigsty you find yourself in now. God is the God of the second chance, of the seventy times seven chances. His mercies are new every morning[6], and morning is not when the sun rises, but when we wake up to the wonderful good news of God's amazing grace to the world through Jesus.

Know that God is *still* for you

Do you remember the blessings and benefits that Paul lists in Romans chapter eight? One of them was, "*If God is for us, who can be against us?*"[7] And God *is* for you. When we are weak, and have even failed, God the Holy Spirit is there to help you in your weakness. To pray again. To come back to him again.

Being restored back to the presence of the Lord

When Peter realised his failure, "*he went outside and wept bitterly*".[8] This is such a vivid picture of Satan's plan for every human being,

4 Luke 22:62
5 Jeremiah 29:11
6 Lamentations 3:23
7 Romans 8:31
8 Luke 22:62 NIV

to be separated with deep pain and regret from God our Father. The goal of repentance is always being restored to God's presence through the removal of sin, guilt, shame, condemnation. Consider these promises:

> *So now there is no condemnation for those who belong to Christ Jesus. And because you belong to him, the power of the life-giving Spirit has freed you from the power of sin that leads to death.*[9]
>
> *Now repent of your sins and turn to God, so that your sins may be wiped away. Then times of refreshment will come from the presence of the Lord.*[10]
>
> *So let us come boldly to the throne of our gracious God. There we will receive his mercy, and we will find grace to help us when we need it most.*[11]

A prophetic sense I have for you, dear reader

As I was writing these words, I sensed a strong leading by the Holy Spirit to tell you that Jesus is *for* you—much more, even, than you ever will desire to be for him. Please don't interpret this message of having an unfailing faith as being all about how strong your faith muscle is, and how hard you can grit your teeth with self-discipline to hold on. He wants you to know that his love and passion for you is so much greater than yours could ever be for him. He loved you in this world so much that he gave his only son, and he still does.

He is praying for you right now that your faith will not fail and that you will be restored to your purpose. He did this for Peter, and will do this for you.

9 Romans 8:1-2
10 Acts 3:19-20
11 Hebrews 4:16

Peter's restoration journey

It is interesting to follow Peter's journey both to the cross, and after the cross. Matthew, Mark and Luke all record how Peter *"followed at a distance"* the closer Jesus got to the cross,[12] until his faith finally failed as he denied his Lord. Yet after the cross Luke records how, at the news of the empty tomb, *"Peter jumped up and ran to the tomb to look"*.[13]

Then John records how Peter meets Jesus for breakfast on a beach. They had not yet said a single word to each other since Peter left the courtyard weeping bitterly at the realisation of his denial. His faith had failed under the pressure of the high priest's courtyard, but now it was being restored through a deeply intimate and soul-searching encounter with his Lord on a beach. Jesus focussed the conversation on what was the most important question: *"Do you love me?"* This took the conversation to the heart of the matter as revealed in the first commandment:

> *Love the Lord your God with all your heart, with all your soul, and with all your mind. This is the greatest and most important command.*[14]

God is more interested in what's in your heart than in your head. Without love we are nothing. Love is most important to God, but we don't love God with our own love. Love is not that we first have loved him, but that he first loved us.[15] By the Holy Spirit we receive his "agápē" unconditional, sacrificial love poured out into our hearts.[16] This transforms us to overflow with his love, to him and to the world around us. Jesus first restored Peter to his love, and then commissioned him to his purpose to *"go and feed my sheep"*.[17] What Jesus

12 Luke 22:54
13 Luke 24:12
14 Matthew 22:37-39 CSB
15 1 John 4:10
16 Romans 5:5 NIV
17 John 21:17

had prophesied was fulfilled as Peter went on to *"strengthen [his] brothers"*[18] in an incredible way.

Restored to purpose

It's one thing to believe and receive forgiveness, but often we feel disqualified because of our past, and we struggle with the promise of a future and a hope. Please don't settle for that. Your faith may have failed, but you are not a failure.

Jesus spoke hope and purpose into Peter's future, prophesying to him: *"And you, when you have turned back, strengthen your brothers."*[19] Jesus saw Peter's future purpose, and what a future it turned out to be! Peter was chosen as the preacher on the Day of Pentecost. He was a key leader in the New Testament church Jesus was building. He even wrote two letters that were included in the canon of scripture. Not bad for someone who denied his Lord three times instead of standing with him in that crucial hour.

Yes, our faith may fail. But like Peter, faith can also be restored.

Like the disciples, we can ask Jesus: *"Lord, increase our faith."*[20]

Like Abraham in the midst of what seemed a total impossibility, we can be *"strengthened in faith"*, even when the circumstances want to weaken it.[21]

Faith can be restored and come to you again through hearing the Word of God.

My prayer for you

On the morning of writing this chapter my Bible REAPing (see the toolkit at the end of this book for an explanation of this term) was in 1 Thessalonians 3:2-3, where Paul writes to the church about sending Timothy to them as a helper to strengthen and encourage their faith in the face of their trials:

18 Luke 22:32
19 Luke 22:32 NIV
20 Luke 17:5 KJV
21 Romans 4:20 NIV

> *And we sent Timothy, our brother and God's servant ... to strengthen and establish and to exhort and comfort and encourage you in your faith, that no one [of you] should be disturbed and beguiled and led astray by these afflictions and difficulties.*[22]

My prayer is you would reach out to one or two "Timothys" in your life today who will do this for you. And that you will also experience the very active help of God the Holy Spirit, our great Helper.

PAUSE TO THINK AND TALK ABOUT IT

⇒ What is the one thing that you found most relevant or helpful in this chapter?

⇒ Has your faith ever failed like Peter's? Recall or share your experience.

⇒ Can you recall an experience where someone like Timothy strengthened your faith in the face of a trial?

---

22 Amplified Bible, Classic Edition

CHAPTER SIX

No!

No, in all these things we are more than conquerors through him who loved us[1]

- THE APOSTLE PAUL -

This is a chapter about a short but very powerful and important word in every fight for your faith.

Following Paul's question of whether anything will be able to separate us from the love of Christ, he continues with a powerful declaration, which in many English translations starts with just one word: *No!*

> *No, in all these things we are more than conquerors through him who loved us.*

No is a very powerful word. It draws a line which is not to be crossed. It declares *this far and no further*. As Paul considered "all these things" that he had just listed as potential threats to separate the believer of the love of Christ—trouble, hardship, persecution, hunger, destitution, danger, death—he looked them square in the eye and declared: "*No*, you will not separate me! You have no power or attraction to separate me from my God. Satan, you cannot have my faith. It's a firm *no* from me!"

Paul was clear and decided about what he would not trade his faith for. He had firmly concluded that not everything in life is

1 Romans 8:37 NIV

equally valuable, and the clearer you become about what that is for you, the stronger your *no* will be. You have to decide what you are going to say *yes* to and *no* to.

Scripture is filled with guidance that shows us how our choices in different situations either help or hinder our life and peace. Consider the following, for example:

> *Choose this day whom you will serve.*[2]
>
> *No one can serve two masters.*[3]
>
> *When you love the world, you do not have the love of the Father in you.*[4]

You cannot love God and this world. Which of these are you saying *yes* to and *no* to at the moment?

It's time to decide

Many people have a weak *no* because they have weak convictions of what they have said *yes* to in life. A weak, lukewarm, half-hearted faith is guaranteed to produce a weak, half-hearted *no*. Until you decide what is truly valuable to you, you will always be vulnerable to being deceived under pressure to give up the greater for the lesser in life.

We know that trials will come to many areas of our lives. To our health, finances, employment, relationships, and more. Yet as precious as these are, they are not as valuable as our peace, hope, joy and faith in God. These greater things must become our true treasures and not options for trading in our dealing with the devil and this world's troubles. You could mess with my money, but you can't have my peace. You could batter my body with sickness and disease, but you can't have my hope. You could try to destroy and divide my relationships, but don't think for a minute that I will give

2 Joshua 24:15 ESV
3 Matthew 6:24
4 1 John 2:15

you my joy! You could threaten my very life, but *no*! None of these things are worth giving up the treasure of my faith for.

Don't be someone who is winning the battle in your bank account, but at the same time losing the fight for your faith. Or trying to fill yourself with the pleasures of this world, while running on empty in your spirit. Make a decision today that you will not love this world nor the things of this world, but you will set your mind on the things of the Spirit instead. That's where true life and peace come from, which is more valuable than anything this world can offer you.

Choosing who and what is most important to you is crucial to being able to have a strong *no* to temptation, pressure, compromise, deceit—and ultimately to the question whether you will let any or all of these things drive a wedge between you and God, separating you from his love. To all of this I plead with you to take a strong stand and declare a firm NO. Not just to some of these things some of the time. In all things all the time. No!

In the next chapter we look at what really gives us the power to say *no*. And no, it's not your willpower, but a much greater power that is available to every believer: the power of the victory of the cross.

PAUSE TO THINK AND TALK ABOUT IT

⇒ What is the one thing that you found most relevant or helpful or challenging in this chapter?

⇒ Can you list what is most important to you?

⇒ What are you attributing too much value to in this season?

⇒ Is there something threatening and testing your faith right now? Are you ready to say a firm no to it? What makes this difficult for you, and why?

CHAPTER SEVEN

Being more than a conqueror

In all these things we are more than conquerors through him who loved us[1]

- THE APOSTLE PAUL -

In every spiritual battle it is crucial for you to understand that you are *not* the hero of the story, and specifically to this chapter, that you are not the conqueror. But you are *more than* a conqueror. This is the single most empowering revelation of your identity in Jesus that will transform the way you position yourself in every trial against every spiritual force of hell set against you.

If you think that you have to be the stronger one in the battle, then any victory will depend on you. But this is not how we take our stand against the evil one. No, the good news is that there is a Great Conqueror *through whom* you can overcome in every trial and trouble you face. You are enabled to stand in his strength for your victory.

Be strong in the Lord and in his mighty power.[2]

Jesus is the Great Conqueror, and the conquest Paul refers to is the victory of the cross where Jesus won the battle against all

1 Romans 8:37 NIV

2 Ephesians 6:10

spiritual forces, darkness and wickedness. Jesus triumphed over sin and hell and death through his death, burial and resurrection.

We have a new "hypernikáō" identity through Christ

In the original text, the phrase *"more than conquerors"* is actually one word, *hypernikáō*, which is made up of two parts: the prefix hypér (meaning "beyond, excessive, more than") and then nikáō (meaning to conquer, be victorious, overcome, prevail, subdue, carry off the victory, especially in battle).

Together this word declares a powerful new identity that the believer has in Christ: I am a hyper-conqueror in Christ, completely and overwhelmingly victorious in battle. Through him who loved me, I am the benefactor of his exceeding victory on the cross. The benefits and blessings of the resurrection transfer from the cross to me and then through me into any circumstance that I face — no matter how terrible or confusing. I am more than a conqueror through Christ who loves me!

His victory is my victory

When you understand and believe that what he did on the cross he did for you, then his victory works through him to you, and you become more than a conqueror.

This battle is not about you versus the devil. This is about the Lord Jesus Christ versus the devil. He won the battle, and you get the benefits. Because of Jesus' victory on the cross, you also can be victorious in your battle. When you believe *in* him, you can have victory *through* him.

It is not just about you trying to survive in and against *all these struggles*, but about you standing in your position as more than a conqueror, trusting that the victory and power of the Great Conqueror will show up in every circumstance and trial that you face in this life.

You are not the conqueror.
The devil is not the conqueror.
Circumstances will not be the conqueror.
Cancer will not be the conqueror in my life!
I will be healed, either in this life or the next.

No, despite all these things, overwhelming victory is ours through Christ, who loved us.[3]

Early on after my diagnosis as I woke up one morning, I sensed the Holy Spirit say to me: "*Wolfi, cancer will not determine your destiny, only I will.*" I still believe this.

I am more than a conqueror over cancer. This is the position I take as I face these brutal medical facts by faith in the God who is the Great Conqueror.

Becoming "fully persuaded" in your faith

It's one thing to have a new identity of being more than a conqueror in Christ, but next Paul calls us into a process of becoming fully persuaded and confident to establish our faith on foundations that will not fail, no matter what trials we may face along the way.

In the rest of the book we will consider how that process happens, and the various areas on which we establish an unwavering, fully persuaded faith that does not fail.

3 Romans 8:37

PAUSE TO THINK AND TALK ABOUT IT

⇒ What is the one thing that you found most relevant or helpful in this chapter?

⇒ Describe in your own words how you understand your new "more than conqueror" identity, and what it means to you.

⇒ What difference does this revelation make to the way you face trials in this life?

⇒ Explain what you understand by the statement that, "You are not the a conqueror, but you are *more than* a conqueror."

CHAPTER EIGHT

Becoming fully persuaded

For I am fully persuaded / convinced
that nothing can ever separate us from God's love[1]
- THE APOSTLE PAUL -

Paul declares that Abraham was *fully persuaded* in his faith:

> *He did not waver in unbelief at God's promise but was strengthened in his faith and gave glory to God, because he was fully convinced that what God had promised, he was also able to do.*[2]

What do you really believe *"without wavering"*? What are the non-negotiables of your faith?

What are you fully convinced and persuaded about as you take your stand in the struggles and trials you face in life?

In this chapter we will understand what it means for us to have an *unwavering and fully persuaded faith* like Abraham did.

Becoming fully persuaded is not something we can just *get*, but something we *grow* in our lives. Our faith persuasion is a step by step process that includes moving us from *intellectual persuasion* about what we believe, to an experiential knowledge by which you become convinced to the point where you are fully persuaded of

1 Romans 8:38
2 Romans 4:20-21 CSB

what you confess to believe about God: that he is trustworthy, and that he can and will do what he has promised.

Jesus describes this process as *"remaining in me, and my words remaining (or abiding) in you"*:

> *But if you remain in me and my words remain in you, you may ask for anything you want, and it will be granted!*[3]

To remain or abide means to stay, to wait, to marinade, with the result that you become *inseparable from* or one with, something, or someone. The 18th century German protestant theologian Leopold Rückert, in his book *Das Abendmahl*, describes the result of abiding as *"when something has established itself permanently within my soul, and always exerts its power in me"*.[4]

It's the process by which the Word of God moves from the words of the Bible all the way to *"let[ting] the message about Christ, in all its richness, fill your lives."*[5] It's the result of the pursuit of knowing Christ and the power of his resurrection.[6]

Eugene Peterson, the author of The Message version of the Bible, called this *"long obedience in the same direction"* in his book with this title[7]. Becoming persuaded is the result of all the faith inputs accumulating into your life, similar to going to the gym and building up your strength with every workout session. With every exercise of a spiritual discipline, your faith persuasion is strengthened.

When you go to your Bible again.
When you turn back to God in prayer.
When you recommit to restore fellowship with other believers.
When you choose another fast.
When you resist a temptation.

3 John 15:7
4 *Das Abendmahl* by Leopold Emanuel Rückert
5 Colossians 3:16
6 Philippians 3:10 NIV
7 *A Long Obedience in the Same Direction—Discipleship in an Instant Society* by Eugene H. Peterson

When you show up to serve with your gifts.
When you honour God with your possessions and giving.
When you step out to share the good news another time.
When you make yourself available to help someone grow as a follower of Jesus.
When you choose to obey what he instructs, like forgiving someone, or repenting of pride.
When you choose to turn back to trusting God again after a disappointment.
When you come back to trust Jesus after your faith has failed.
When you choose love over hate, hope over despair, faith over fear.
When you pray again, trust again, hope again, believe again.
Persuasion develops when you stay long enough to see God working in his timing.
When you open your Bible one more time, pray again, and do it all over again.
That is discipleship: *long obedience in the same direction.*

It's similar to what M. Craig Barnes[8] called *The Leadership Law of Gravitas* when considering what makes leaders weighty, worthy and believable:

> *Gravitas is a condition of the soul that has developed enough spiritual mass to attract other souls. It makes the soul appear old, but gravitas has nothing to do with age. It has everything to do with scars that have healed well, failures that have been redeemed, sins that have been forgiven, and thorns that have settled into the flesh.*

8 Christianity Today, Sept 2005 online

Becoming persuaded through experience

Through this process of abiding, we grow a persuaded faith that is resilient against the trials life brings to us. We experience the fruit of faith that confirms that God and his Word are fully trustworthy.

Do you remember my definition of resurrection faith in chapter three? That faith is fully trusting God—his greatness, wisdom and goodness—in everything at all times, and being fully convinced that he is able to do what he has promised.

This is the faith Paul, Abraham and Mary had as they all believed that the Lord was able to and *"would do what he said"*.[9] They believed in the power of God's Word, that created this world with *"let there be"*.

I believe you too can have such a fully persuaded faith through the Lord Jesus Christ.

> A faith that is founded on God's unshakable word and promises.
> A faith that carries you through whatever challenges and temptations this life throws at you.
> A faith that fully trusts God no matter what, even if you don't understand what God is doing or not doing.
> A faith that does not change when circumstances change.
> A faith that cannot be separated by anything or anyone from the love of God which is in Jesus Christ our Lord.

The power of our words, testimony and attitude

Words are great carriers of power, and there is life and death in the power of the tongue[10]. The words we speak create the world we live in, and we must make sure the words of our testimony align with our faith, not drifting into doubting or double-mindedness.

Note how the scriptures[11] declare that the apostles firstly *"defeated Satan"* by the blood of the Lamb (by what Jesus accomplished on the cross), then secondly *"by the word of their testimony"*

9 Luke 1:45
10 Proverbs 18:21
11 Revelation 12:11

(giving all glory to God), and thirdly they did not love their lives so much that they were afraid to die. This describes their attitude, meaning how they positioned themselves in life in relation to a circumstance they were facing.

In the next chapters you will see how crucial these are for having a faith that does not fail.

Paul's testimony of God's supernatural deliverance

Paul's own testimony to the Corinthian believers about how God delivered him is incredibly bold and encouraging. Have a slow read through his testimony below and see how boldly he trusts God, not hesitant to face the brutal facts of his trial, nor to testify of how God had delivered them even when they expected to die. Notice how Paul values their prayers as part of what God has done to deliver him from death.

> *We think you ought to know, dear brothers and sisters, about the trouble we went through in the province of Asia. We were crushed and overwhelmed beyond our ability to endure, and we thought we would never live through it. In fact, we expected to die. But as a result, we stopped relying on ourselves and learned to rely only on God, who raises the dead. And he did rescue us from mortal danger, and he will rescue us again. We have placed our confidence in him, and he will continue to rescue us. And you are helping us by praying for us. Then many people will give thanks because God has graciously answered so many prayers for our safety.*[12]

Growing your persuasion through the testimonies of others

My faith for healing has also been encouraged by many testimonies I have heard about and witnessed. Even the fact that I am still able to write here two and a half years after the original grim

12 2 Corinthians 1:8-11

prognosis is something of a miracle, or at least at great odds with what was expected.

Three weeks ago here in London, Deb Olivier, one of our leaders who is a secondary school biology teacher, experienced a quite extraordinary healing. Over lunch with another couple from church, John and Liz Henderson, Deb mentioned that she had for months been suffering tremendous pain and limited arm movement due to a frozen shoulder. If you've ever had that condition, or known someone who has, it really is a debilitating issue. John offered to pray for healing and as they laid their hands on Deb's shoulder, she felt a warmth come over her shoulder, and immediately the pain left. John asked her to test the movement, and Deb raised her arm right back to normal reach, without any pain at all. I saw Deb again this week, three weeks later, and she was still ecstatic to show me how she was able to lift and move her arm with full range and pain free. God does heal in response to prayer.

Over these past two years, I have regularly read testimonies recorded in the book *Miracles Today*,[13] in which the author demonstrates that miraculous works of God have been part of the experience of the church around the world since Christianity began and that they continue into the present. It includes many accounts of documented healings from cancer, which of course is so encouraging to me.

But let's be honest

While there are many convincing accounts of healing from cancer and other terminal illnesses, there are also many tragic accounts of those who have not been healed. It would be a denial of reality to say that most of us, even if we believe in supernatural healing, don't also know someone who believed and prayed for healing just as I am, and yet they are still ill, or have died. Cancer and disease do seem to win sometimes. Even often. Sickness and circumstances

13 *Miracles Today: The Supernatural Work of God in the Modern World* by Craig S. Keener

don't always turn around in response to our faith and prayer. Those are just brutal facts we have to honestly face.

Just a few days ago I spoke with a friend whose father-in-law recently died of a brain tumour just like mine. They believed and prayed as we do, yet he died.

Some are healed. Some are not. Some receive what can only be described as a miracle, while others suffer miserably on their deathbed.

What do we do with this tension of faith? How do we have a faith that does not fail despite the questions and often confusing outcomes? Why are some healed, and others not? Why does it seem that sometimes faith *"works"*, and at other times not?

You can imagine that my friend whose father-in-law died of brain cancer is severely conflicted as he is now trying to remain in faith for my healing of the same condition. Will God heal this time or not? If he does heal me, then why did he not heal his father-in-law too? What can I really, fully trust God for and with?

Recently I noticed that someone had stopped attending our church services and when I inquired, I was told that she was angry with God because her father had recently died of cancer. He had not been healed as she had believed and prayed that he would be. I haven't seen her again since. This seems a tragic failure of faith, in which the circumstances have caused her to doubt God and separate her from his love.

There's a lot at stake with this

You will never build a persuaded faith without finding a satisfying way to accept this tension. At worst some may quit their faith entirely, while others may settle for a "whatever happens, happens", "*que sera sera,* whatever will be will be" kind of cheerful, pessimistic faith. Others may at best be left with a cynical or a double-minded faith, while still others get stuck in the paralysis of analysis, never getting past asking *why*.

It should be obvious that none of these responses to our trials are what the apostle had in mind when speaking about a fully persuaded faith that does not fail. I am convinced that this is indeed possible, and is what Ali and I have been experiencing through this cancer trial.

My sincere hope for your future faith

In the next few chapters, I will explain what I have come to understand as the difference between faith in the mysteries of healing, versus faith in certainties of the gospel and its firm foundations. Processing the brutal cancer facts through this wisdom from the Lord has helped me to face these challenges with unshakable confidence through these past two and a half years. I can confidently confess that through this, my faith has grown more and more persuaded with unwavering foundations.

My sincere hope is that the wisdom and truth that I get to share with you will complete an impartation of the gift that the Holy Spirit intended for you to receive—the gift of *faith that does not fail.*

PAUSE TO THINK AND TALK ABOUT IT

⇒ What is the one thing that you found most relevant or helpful in this chapter?

⇒ What do you struggle with most when considering "long obedience in the same direction"?

⇒ Reflect back on the "Leadership Law of Gravitas". How do you recognise that in your life?

CHAPTER NINE

The mysteries and the certainties of faith

This Christian life is a great mystery, far exceeding our understanding, but some things are clear enough[1]

- THE APOSTLE PAUL -

As I start writing this chapter, I am still facing the brutal medical facts of my cancer diagnosis, having been told that I only have two or three months to live, perhaps only a few weeks.

Facing this reality

This chapter presents the wisdom that the Lord gave me to process and face my cancer challenge, which is that *there are mysteries of faith, and there are certainties of faith, and that a faith that does not fail is built on the eternal certainties of the gospel—even while we also trust God fully in the mystery areas of our faith according to what we believe he has revealed to us.*

This approach has been key for me to have both great peace about God's hand working his will in and through my situation, as

1 1 Timothy 3:16 The Message

well as enabling me to stay strong in faith for the promises I believe he has given me for healing. I am praying that this will help you too, because it could make the difference between your faith flourishing or failing.

> *The strength of your faith is determined by the foundations on which you build it.*

Faith for miracles in the mysteries

I am still convinced that God can heal me and that my life can be preserved for many years to come for the sake of fulfilling his purposes for my life. I have this conviction not by blind faith or wishful thinking, but from his written revealed Word that says God is the Healer.

My faith confession, based on these convictions, is that I will live and not die, and I will continue to fulfil his purposes which are not yet done in my life.

Note, however, that these specific confessions from God's Word are as I have felt led to pray and believe in this circumstance. Every believer can hear God's voice for themselves and discern his will and ways in their specific situation, in accordance with revelation from scripture. At the end of this book, there's a practical section on how to grow your faith convictions through REAPing the Bible—a method I use to richly engage with God's Word.

Wisdom is needed

It's one thing to face your trials and even endure through them and find purpose in the pain. But without resolving the questions you have about them, the apostle James—directly after his encouragement to *"consider it pure joy... whenever you face trials"*[2]—warns that you may end up being *"like a wave of the sea that is blown and tossed by the wind... double-minded and unstable in all you*

2 James 1:2 NIV

do".[3] That's quite a picture of what trials can do to faith, and James instructs that the antidote to this double-mindedness is to ask God for *wisdom.*

Wisdom is the antidote to a double-minded faith.

Walking by faith and wisdom

When I first received the cancer diagnosis, I asked the Lord firstly to give me strength to *walk by faith* in and through this trial, and secondly that I would *walk in wisdom* as I face the mystery of divine healing.

As I have stated above, I am believing to be healed of this cancer. Scripture declares that part of our new covenant through the blood of Jesus is healing for the body, for: *"By his stripes we are healed."*[4] Yet I am conscious that many others have believed in a similar way to us, but have died. To say that God *always* heals in response to faith in his Word is simply not true. Therefore I must conclude that *healing is a mystery, not a certainty.* I am often reminded of a quote by the apologist Amy Orr-Ewing, drawn from the words of a dying member of her congregation: *"A miracle is God's to give, not ours to take."*[5]

A mark of a mature faith is to accept that God is God, and we are not. There are some things we simply will not understand. The Kingdom is now, and is also still to come. Healing is for here and now, but will be perfected in heaven. Some will be resurrected from the dead in this life, but we will all die sometime. Even Lazarus died again.

Accepting that healing is a mystery does not mean that I do not or cannot have great faith for healing. In fact, it frees me from needing to fully understand what is not possible to fully understand. It enables my feet to be planted on the solid rock of the eternal

3 James 1:6-8 NIV

4 Isaiah 53:5 NKJV

5 *Where Is God In All The Suffering?* by Amy Orr-Ewing

certainties of my faith, and from that position to believe my Lord for miracles even in the mysteries.

Because I am fully persuaded that God is great, good and wise, I can — like Paul — fully trust God even in the mystery, declaring that:

> *We know that God causes everything to work together for the good of those who love God and are called according to his purpose for them.*[6]

We can and do have faith for healing, but this is not the foundation of our faith. We don't build on the mysteries, but on the eternal certainties.

Building your faith on the eternal certainties you are persuaded about

A faith that does not fail is built on the solid foundation of the undeniable facts of eternal certainties you are fully persuaded about from scripture. As a follower of Jesus it is crucial to become fully persuaded about your personal biblical convictions and beliefs, and then live confidently based on what you believe. In the previous chapter we saw how we become fully persuaded through the process of abiding in Jesus, and his Word abiding in us. As we do this, our personal biblical convictions are shaped and we become more and more fully persuaded about the truths that form the solid foundation on which we build our fully convinced faith.

Peter, whose faith failed in the face of a question when he denied knowing Jesus, would later in his letter instruct believers: *"Always be prepared to give an answer to everyone who asks you to give the reason for the hope that you have."*[7] He recognised the importance of being confident and persuaded about what we believe as a foundation of a faith that will not fail.

What we believe will determine how we live, and whether our faith will remain resiliently firm or will fail.

6 Romans 8:28

7 1 Peter 3:15 NIV

In Romans chapter eight, where Paul poses the big "what will separate us from God's love" question, I see at least five eternal certainties on which Paul built his fully persuaded, unfailing faith. These are:

1. Being persuaded about the gift of eternal life
2. Being persuaded that God is Love
3. Being persuaded about the resurrected Lord Jesus Christ
4. Being persuaded that to live is Christ
5. Being persuaded that to die is gain

Moving Martha from the mystery to certainty

We will look at each of these separately in the next five chapters, but first, one more lesson from Martha as she wrestled with the mystery of her brother's death.

Martha had sent Jesus a message that, *"Lord, the one you love is sick."* Her expectation was that Jesus would rush over straight away and heal her brother Lazarus, but for some reason we see that *"although Jesus loved Martha, Mary, and Lazarus, he stayed where he was for the next two days"*.[8] Lazarus died and had been in the tomb for four days by the time Jesus finally arrived, and we understandably find Martha full of questions and confusion: *"Lord, if only you had been here, my brother would not have died."*[9] You could say that she was stuck on the mystery of Jesus' timing as well as his apparent unwillingness to save her brother, and this even though he loved him. As she wrestles with these questions, Jesus lifts her focus from the *mystery* she cannot understand, to the *certainty* of the greater resurrection truth:

> *I am the resurrection and the life. Anyone who believes in me will live, even after dying. Everyone who lives in me and believes in me will never ever die.*[10]

8 John 11:5-6
9 John 11:21
10 John 11:25-26

Then Jesus asks the crucial question: *"Do you believe this, Martha?"*

Her answer to this question will determine whether she stays stuck in the mystery of what she does not understand, or chooses to build her faith on what is an eternal certainty.

This was her response: *"'Yes, Lord,' she replied, 'I believe that you are the Messiah, the Son of God, who is to come into the world.'"*

Now her faith was no longer based on the mystery of Jesus' timing and whether or not her brother would be raised from the dead, but rather on who Jesus is, and on the certainty of the resurrection to eternal glory. She has moved from being shaken by the mystery to standing firm on the certainty of the gospel.

Considering what you are fully persuaded about

What do you really believe? What are the certainties of your faith? What do you believe irrespective of your circumstances? What have you concluded to be eternal truths by which you will live or even die?

PAUSE TO THINK AND TALK ABOUT IT

⇒ What is the one thing that you found most relevant or helpful in this chapter?

⇒ What "mystery" of faith are you wrestling with at the moment?

⇒ Do you, like Martha, struggle with a question of, "Lord, if only you had..."? What is your question?

⇒ Read the answer Jesus gave Martha in John 11:25-26. Do you believe this?

CHAPTER TEN

Being persuaded about death and eternity

Everyone who believes in him will not perish
but have eternal life[1]
- THE APOSTLE JOHN -

If you were to die today, are you certain about what awaits you in eternity, or is it a mystery to you?

When was the last time you thought deeply about what happens when we die? Or about what awaits us in eternity beyond the grave? Are we just destined for nothingness, dust to dust, some type of reincarnation, perfection, judgement, heaven, or hell? We know that we will all die sometime. Some sooner than others. Some prematurely, unexpectedly, tragically. Some naturally—perhaps still tragically. The question is: what do you believe about when that day comes?

> *And now, dear brothers and sisters, we want you to know what will happen to the believers who have died so you will not grieve or mourn like people who have no hope.*[2]

1 John 3:16b
2 1 Thessalonians 4:13

The apostle Paul declares that *"neither death nor life"* would separate us from the love of God. He had a fully persuaded faith about eternity that would not fail even when he faced the threat of death, or death itself. Let's have a look at what the scripture teaches about death and eternity, and then consider the question: *Are you fully persuaded that even death will not separate you from God nor cause your faith to fail?*

Facing death and eternity

These questions became real to me very quickly after my initial cancer diagnosis. Death was staring me in the face. One of the first exercises I did then was to consider what I really believed about life after death. Was I fully persuaded about what I had been confessing and preaching for so long, or was it just a mental assent kind of faith about this subject?

I concluded this crucial question with a resounding *"Yes, I am fully persuaded that by grace through faith in Jesus Christ I have the gift of eternal life!"* By removing any doubt or mystery, this eternal perspective of life has become an unshakable foundation throughout my challenging cancer journey, while facing the prospect of my imminent death. I have no fear of death, but a supernatural peace and even excitement that *"to die is (will be) gain!"*[3]

> *Even when walking through the dark valley of death,*
> *I will not be afraid, for you are close beside me.*[4]

What the Bible teaches about death and eternity

The Bible reveals God as eternal, from *"In the beginning"* to *"forever"*, and we humans are created in his eternal image. It opens our eyes to see beyond the horizons of this natural world and the short life we have on earth. It teaches about eternal life, the resurrection

3 Philippians 1:21 NIV
4 Psalm 23:4 TLB

from the dead, eternal judgement, heaven or hell, and finally a new heaven and earth which the old apostle John describes like this:

> *I heard a loud shout from the throne, saying, "Look, God's home is now among his people! He will live with them, and they will be his people. God himself will be with them. He will wipe every tear from their eyes, and there will be no more death or sorrow or crying or pain. All these things are gone forever. And the one sitting on the throne said, "Look, I am making everything new!"*[5]

The gospel of eternal life

Our faith is not for this earthly life only. The gospel is not some self improvement program just for a better life now, but rather a message promising the gift of eternal life through faith in Jesus Christ the Lord.

> *For the wages of sin is death, but the free gift of God is eternal life through Christ Jesus our Lord.*[6]
>
> *For God so loved the world that he gave his one and only Son, that whoever believes in him shall not perish but have eternal life.*[7]
>
> *My sheep listen to my voice; I know them, and they follow me. I give them eternal life, and they will never perish.*[8]

The resurrection of Jesus is the foundation of eternal hope

I made the case previously that the resurrection of Jesus is ultimately our source of hope that God is faithful and able to do what he has promised. Jesus simply declares it like this:

5 Revelation 21:3-5
6 Romans 6:23
7 John 3:16 NIV
8 John 10:27-28

> *Since I live, you also will live.*[9]
>
> *I am the resurrection and the life. The one who believes in me, even if he dies, will live.*[10]

If Jesus is not raised from the dead, our faith is in vain. But since he was indeed raised and is alive, we have all the reason for our hope. We will establish this further in the coming chapter on being persuaded about the resurrection and Lordship of Jesus Christ.

A person's response to Jesus in this life will determine their eternal destiny

It's true that many have rejected and many will reject Jesus,[11] but scripture reveals that God has made a way, through Jesus, for everyone to come to him and receive the gift of eternal life. Jesus claimed himself to be the only way to the Father.[12] This is the radically exclusive message of the gospel, but also at the same time *the gospel is radically inclusive for all the world* that God so loved to come to him.

> *For God did not send his Son into the world to condemn the world, but to save the world through him. Anyone who believes in him is not condemned, but anyone who does not believe is already condemned, because he has not believed in the name of the one and only Son of God.*[13]
>
> *God our Saviour wants everyone to be saved and to understand the truth.*[14]

Not believing in Jesus is either a deliberate choice for those who have heard the gospel and rejected it, or it is a case of ignorance, for those who have never heard. How God judges the latter is also a mystery, but because we know God is fair and just, we fully trust that

9 John 14:19
10 John 11:25 CSB
11 John 1:11-12
12 John 14:6
13 John 3:17-18 CSB
14 1 Timothy 2:3-4

on the judgement day when *"every knee will bow... and every tongue will confess that Jesus Christ is Lord"*,[15] all will do so acknowledging that God has judged fairly and justly according to each person's response to the revelation of God through Christ, conscience and or creation.

Facing death and eternity

When the apostle Paul was facing the very imminent prospect of death in a Roman jail, he shared his feelings about this in his letter to the disciples in Philippi, stating: *"For to me, living means living for Christ, and dying is even better (or gain)."*

He continues:

> *I don't know which one I should choose.*
> *I am torn between the two.*
> *I long to depart and be with Christ—which is far better*[16]

You can see that for Paul there was a very thin line between this life and the next. He lived in the light of a clear view of eternity, and frequently encouraged disciples to do the same.

Take some time to meditate on the verses below, while considering your personal hope and expectation of eternity:

> *But our citizenship is in heaven. And we eagerly await a Saviour from there, the Lord Jesus Christ.*[17]
>
> *Listen, I tell you a mystery: we will not all sleep, but we will all be changed—in a flash, in the twinkling of an eye, at the last trumpet. For the trumpet will sound, the dead will be raised imperishable, and we will be changed.*[18]
>
> *When Christ, who is your life, appears, then you also will appear with him in glory.*[19]

15 Philippians 2:10-11 CSB
16 Philippians 1:21-23 CSB
17 Philippians 3:20 NIV
18 1 Corinthians 15:51-52 NIV
19 Colossians 3:4 NIV

And now the prize awaits me—the crown of righteousness, which the Lord, the righteous Judge, will give me on the day of his return. And the prize is not just for me but for all who eagerly look forward to his appearing.[20]

He will keep you strong to the end so that you will be free from all blame on the day when our Lord Jesus Christ returns.[21]

Abraham was confidently looking forward to a city with eternal foundations, a city designed and built by God.[22]

A story of a near death experience I had

Many years ago I was involved in an armed robbery. And no, it wasn't me doing the robbery! I was working as project manager on a large construction site and was in the site office with the site manager and an assistant on a Friday afternoon winding down the week. Suddenly two men burst in, wielding guns. They were high on drugs screaming for us to give them the wages, which back then we paid in cash every second Friday. Unfortunately for them, they chose the wrong Friday. Unfortunately for us, this made them even angrier and more aggressive. Soon they had all three of us on the floor, with a pistol rammed into the side of my face. We handed over all valuables we had including the company car keys, and thankfully they made their getaway without harming us.

I tell you this story because of the contrasting responses that were so evident between me and the other two people in this life-threatening ordeal. As I lay on the floor with the gun shoved in my face, I had no fear of death. In fact, I had a supernatural peace and even a strange inner excitement at the possibility of being in the presence of Jesus that day! Yet the others were utterly fearful. They had professed to being believers in Jesus, but in this near death experience, their faith failed as their foundations were shaken.

20 2 Timothy 4:8
21 1 Corinthians 1:8
22 Hebrews 11:10

How would you react in such a situation? How clear is your view of eternity as you live this present life? Do you long for his return, or merely consider this a possibility?

No fear of death

A persuaded, unfailing faith faces death without fear and boldly declares: *Death, I do not fear you. You have no power over me. I am fully convinced that I have the gift of eternal life, and therefore death is just a doorway for me to the eternal presence of my Lord and Saviour!*

I will be in the presence of our Lord!

Paul also wrote that he would much prefer *"to be absent from the body and to be at home with the Lord".*[23] I have at times joked that for those of us who love experiencing God's *presence* there is a guaranteed way to do so, which is to die! But seriously: this is what we "gain" in death—God's real eternal presence. Wow.

Friends, when I die, whenever and however that will be, please know that I am in the eternal presence of my Lord and Saviour. Yes, do miss me and mourn me, but do so as those who share a confident, persuaded hope of the gift of eternal life.

As for you, I pray that you will be and remain fully persuaded about death and the gift of eternal life, and with that as a foundation truth you will build your unfailing faith—even in the face of death or the threat of death.

Next, let's consider the certainty we can have about the love of God.

23 2 Corinthians 5:8 Amplified Bible

PAUSE TO THINK AND TALK ABOUT IT

⇒ What is the one thing that you found most relevant or helpful in this chapter?

⇒ Imagine being in a similar situation to me when we were being robbed at gunpoint. How do you think you would have reacted? Why?

⇒ Does the idea of being in God's real eternal presence excite you? If not, why?

CHAPTER ELEVEN

Being persuaded about God's unchanging love and goodness

God is love[1]

- THE APOSTLE JOHN -

Does God love you? How do you know?

Your persuasion about God's unchanging love and goodness is the next crucial foundation for a faith that does not fail.

This was the central issue at the root of the very first temptation in the Garden, and the cause for the first failure of faith recorded in the Bible. When the serpent tempted Adam and Eve, he did not try to convince them that God was not real, but instead he slithered into their lives with a strategy to undermine their trust in God by misrepresenting and distorting his character to them.

> *Did God really say?* (Challenging God's Word)
> *You will surely not die* (Undermining God's truthfulness)
> *God knows that when you eat ... you will be like God*[2] (Questioning God's motive)

1 1 John 4:8b
2 Genesis 3:1-5

Once they had received these seeds of doubt from the father of lies about God's goodness and trustworthiness, they were vulnerable to the temptation they had been set up for.

> *So she took some of the fruit and ate it ... and he ate it,too.*[3]

Their faith failed because the serpent had managed to distort their understanding of God's nature, *that he is not good, that he cannot be trusted, that he is not for them, and that he does not love them.* From them we see that there is a direct correlation between the strength of our faith and the persuasion we have about God's true nature, and that our faith is weakened and vulnerable by any doubt of his love and goodness towards us.

> *What you know and believe about God will determine how you relate to him.*

The above is a key statement we make in The Follow Course, which I created to help people grow as followers of Jesus. It states an obvious principle, right? If you believe something false about God (or anyone, for that matter), you will never relate to them like you could or should. Sadly, most people today have a very distorted view of who God is and what he is like, so my persuasion is that any new follower of Jesus needs instruction on "knowing God" in order to correct all the lies and deception that the serpent still sows into the gardens of people's minds to separate them from God and his love.

God is love

While there are of course many wonderful and very important things to know about God and what he is like, I am persuaded that every believer or prospective believer must know and believe what I call the essential relational qualities of God. These are that *God is love, God is Father, and God is prodigal*—meaning that he is lavishly abundant with his amazing grace and mercy towards all who come to him. This is exactly how the apostle John summarises

3 Genesis 3:6

this relational nature of God as he writes in his later letter as a wiser old man:

> *See what great love the Father has lavished on us, that we should be called children of God! And that is what we are!*[4]

John also reveals that *"God IS love."*[5]

Love is not merely one of God's attributes. It is intrinsic to his very nature. He doesn't just *have* love, he ***is*** love. This means that everything God does is rooted in and expresses love. God's love is referred to as "agápē" love, which is the selfless, sacrificial, unconditional and enduring love that defines his actions. His love is not based on the worthiness of the recipient but is given freely and abundantly by God's amazing grace. Of course, we see the embodiment of *God is love* in the person of Jesus Christ, and what an amazing, lavish love that is!

God is love with no "buts"

Please understand that God's justice, anger, and even wrath are not opposites to his love, but expressions of his love. God *has* anger, but is not by nature angry. I often hear people say things like *"Yes, God is love, BUT he is also just, angry, wrathful, etc"*, as if God is volatile, sometimes being this, sometimes that. God's love does not contradict his capacity for anger towards sin and anyone or anything that deceives and destroys those he loves. In fact, his love demands justice. His anger is a righteous and just response to sin, evil and injustice—an expression of his holy love aimed at the ultimate restoration, reconciliation and freedom through the gospel.

Please know and believe that God is love, and is perfect in his love. You never need to doubt that, but you will have to be very intentionally alert to the serpent's same old strategy to lie and deceive you about God's nature, and especially his love. It's also one thing to have a theological persuasion that God is love, but quite another to

4 1 John 3:1 NIV
5 1 John 4:8b, 16b

believe and be convinced that God loves **you**, especially when you face adverse circumstances and troubles in life. It's at these times that we ask the most important questions:

Does God love me?
How do I know?
How can I be sure?

Look to the cross, not to circumstance

But God showed his great love for us by sending Christ to die for us while we were still sinners.[6]

There is no greater demonstration of God's love than the cross of Jesus Christ. On the cross he stretched out his saving arms and declared *"I love you"* by laying down his life for us. On the cross he declared *"it is finished"*[7] as the penalty of sin and death was settled once and forever. On the cross Jesus stripped Satan of every right to accuse you. On the cross Jesus endured the most horrific of circumstances on our behalf, even to the point of death.

The cross changes everything and is the central event that reveals the profound and selfless nature of God's love for humanity. And for you. Here we see his love that never fails demonstrated and it is always the place believers look to for confirmation that God did and does indeed love us.

Love is the motivation of the gospel

It may help to see that God's love is the *motivation* of the gospel. It is because God so loved the world—you, me and everyone at all times—that he gave his only Son, Jesus.

For God so loved the world that he gave his one and only Son[8]

6 Romans 5:8
7 John 19:30
8 John 3:16 NIV

The gospel is not just *what* God did, but also includes *why* God did it. The *what* is Christ's death on the cross. The *why* is because he loves you. Jesus did not just *die for us.* Jesus died *because God loves us,* and because he desires to reconcile us to relationship with himself. His love is his motivation, and you were his motivation.

Keep your eyes fixed on Jesus

Those who have a faith that does not fail have learnt to shift the focus of their faith from their circumstances to the victory of the cross. This is always a battle: will we look to circumstances, or to the cross as the measure of God's love?

Who and what we fix our eyes on will determine the strength of our faith. Peter experienced this when he had stepped out of the boat and found himself miraculously walking on the water. But when he *"saw the strong wind and the waves"*[9] he was afraid and began to sink. His faith failed when he focused on the storm, but we can learn from him and from the writer of the book of Hebrews:

> *Let us run with endurance the race God has set before us. We do this by keeping our eyes fixed on Jesus, the champion who initiates and perfects our faith. Because of the joy awaiting him, he endured the cross, disregarding its shame. Now he is seated in the place of honour beside God's throne.*[10]

To *"fix your eyes"* here means *"looking away from all else, and fix them on something".*[11] Those with a persuaded faith that does not fail turn their focus away from their circumstances — whether good or bad — and fix their eyes on Jesus' love demonstrated on the cross. We can do this because the love of God has been, and will always be, most clearly demonstrated through the cross.

Whether things are going well or not, circumstances can never confirm God's love to you like you need it. Whether I am healed, or

9 Matthew 14:30
10 Hebrews 12:1-2
11 Strong's NT 872

not, is not the evidence for, or against, God's love for me. Healing from cancer would be an amazing blessing and miracle, but that alone is not enough to confirm God's love for me. Why not? Because there will always be some other trouble to face. If I say my healing must be because God loves me, then what will I say when new trouble arrives – that God must now love me less? Surely not!

The only evidence that irrefutably proves God's love for us is the cross. This is the unfailing love from which nothing can separate us, if we keep our eyes fixed on the One who is the author and perfecter of our faith.

Yes, in this world we will have trouble, but may our tests and troubles never separate us from the love of God demonstrated in the Lord Jesus Christ. And if you are struggling with this, let me share a final encouragement with you about being restored by the One who loves you.

Do you love me?

When Jesus met Peter on the beach to restore him, he had just one question which he asked three times: *"Do you love me?"*[12] It's notable and relevant to this chapter that Jesus focused on Peter's *love*, not his faith, because the strength of our faith is very much dependent on whether we are persuaded that God does indeed love us, despite the circumstances and trouble we may be going through.

A closer look at Jesus' question and Peter's answers reveals something very profound which I believe was a key to Peter's restoration, and it may be so for you as well if your faith has failed or is wavering.

In Greek, there are two different words for *love* used in this interchange, namely "agápē" (or "agapaō", when used as a verb), essentially meaning "to love like God loves", and "philía" (or "phileō" as a verb), meaning "affectionate friendship".

Here's how I see this exchange progressing, and notice I have inserted the word "only" to make my point below:

12 John 21:15-17

> Peter, do you *agapaō* me? Lord, I (only) *phileō* you.
> Peter, do you *agapaō* me? Lord, I (only) *phileō* you.
> Peter, do you (only) *phileō* me? Lord, you know everything; you know that I (only) *phileō* you.

One way to understand this interaction is that Jesus was leading Peter to finally recognise his own limitations, admitting that *"you know that I (only) phileō you"*. Jesus had agápē love for Peter, but Peter only had philía love for Jesus.

Peter had been so over-confident in himself when Jesus had warned him of Satan's coming test, but now his faith had failed, and he had come to the end of himself. This is a good place to come to because when we are empty, we are most ready to receive what God has to fill us.

Now Peter was ready to receive everything he needed to fulfil God's call on his life. Not by his own strength, but by the Holy Spirit poured out at Pentecost. And the same Spirit would pour out into Peter's heart the agápē love of God, which is also available for all of us when we need love restored.

> *For we know how dearly God loves (agápē) us, because he has given us the Holy Spirit to fill our hearts with his love (agápē).*[13]

From this promise we see that God agápē loves you, that the Holy Spirit has been given to you, and he will fill your heart with his agápē love. If you need that, just pause right now to ask him, and by faith receive his agápē love filling your heart.

I pray that through every circumstance of life you will remain fully persuaded of God's love for you as demonstrated on the cross, because this is one of the crucial foundations for having a faith that does not fail.

> *Give thanks to the Lord, for he is good;*
> *his faithful love endures forever.*[14]

13 Romans 5:5
14 Psalm 136:1

PAUSE TO THINK AND TALK ABOUT IT

⇒ What is the one thing that you found most relevant or helpful in this chapter?

⇒ What circumstance has most challenged you to question God's love for you?

⇒ Share a situation where you have been able to "fix your eyes on Jesus", shifting your focus from the good or bad circumstance, to only the love demonstrated on the cross.

⇒ Consider what difference adding the *why* of the gospel makes to hearing or sharing a gospel presentation. Why do you think so?

> *The gospel is the good news, that because of God's love for the world—including you—God became man in Jesus Christ. He lived the perfect life we should have lived, without any sin. On the cross he died the death we should have died, in our place for our sin. Three days later he rose from the dead, proving that he was and is the promised Messiah, fully qualified to forgive sin and offer all who would repent and believe the gift of eternal life in his name.*[15]

15 Adapted from the gospel summary in *The Purple Basics: Understanding the Message of the Gospel in the New Testament* by Dr Rice Broocks

CHAPTER TWELVE

Being persuaded about the resurrected Lord Jesus Christ

Who do you say I am?[1]

- JESUS, MESSIAH, THE SON OF THE LIVING GOD -

A faith that does not fail must be fully persuaded that Jesus was crucified, died, was buried, and rose again on the third day, thereby confirming that he is Christ and Lord.

Do you believe that? Why, or why not?

The greater your revelation of who Jesus is, the stronger and more persuaded your faith will be. Jesus is the object of our faith. He is the source of our faith. What we believe about him will determine the strength and resilience of our faith, and whether our faith will fail or flourish.

Jesus is more than just Jesus

When the apostle Paul made his case for having a fully persuaded faith he declared that "*nothing in all creation will ever be able to separate us from the love of God that is revealed in Christ Jesus our*

1 Matthew 16:15b

Lord".[2] Notice that he doesn't just write *"as revealed in Jesus"*, but here intentionally uses the full title of *"as revealed in Christ Jesus our Lord"*.

My first point here is that I am concerned that often we get too familiar with God and in our reductionist language we are in danger of losing or at least minimising the revelation of who Jesus is in his fullness. We pray, *"In the name of Jesus, amen,"* but how aware are we of *who* we are really praying to, and saying *"amen"* to? Do we still know the power of his name, the name above all names?

"Christ" is his title, meaning "Anointed One", from the Greek word "Christos", equivalent to the Hebrew word "Messiah". When you call Jesus "Christ" or "Messiah", you acknowledge that this Jesus of Nazareth is the One prophesied in the Old Testament to be the deliverer and king who would bring salvation to God's people. Jesus is the Christ!

"Lord" is his position, meaning master or ruler, from the Greek word "kýrios". When you call Jesus "Lord", you acknowledge his divinity, his supreme authority over all creation, and your submission to his sovereign rule and leadership over all of your life. Jesus is Lord!

When Peter came to the end of his message on the day of Pentecost, he proclaimed Jesus as being Lord and Messiah:

> *So let everyone in Israel know for certain that God has made this Jesus, whom you crucified, to be both Lord and Messiah!*[3]

This is Jesus who we believe is the incarnate God the Son who became flesh and dwelt among us. This is Jesus through whom the glory of God was revealed to us in fullness. This is Jesus who was crucified and rose again, purchasing forgiveness for all the world. This is Jesus who is alive, ascended and seated at the right hand of God the Father, making intercession for us. This is Jesus whose return to rule and reign we eagerly await. This is Jesus who

2 Romans 8:39

3 Acts 2:36

will judge the living and the dead and establish God's Kingdom fully forever.

Friend, this is Jesus who is both Lord and Christ the Messiah, and because of who he is we believe and are saved.

Do a prayer upgrade

Concerning my earlier point about becoming too familiar with God, may I encourage you to try to intentionally change your words when you pray. Instead of the often mild (lame?) *"Jesus I just want to..."* (why do we even say *"just"*?!), try praying boldly like this: *"Father, I come to you in the name of the Lord Jesus Christ of Nazareth"*, or when you end your prayer declare a bold *"I ask this in the name of the Lord Jesus Christ, amen!"* Do this with deliberate engagement, to remind yourself who the real Jesus is whom you are praying to and trusting in. At the same time you will be reminding every demon that is prowling around like a roaring lion that your Lord is the Greater Lion of the tribe of Judah! I have often said that every Christian should pray at least one violent prayer a day, engaging in the very real battle raging for the hearts and minds of all people. But now back to the resurrection.

The resurrected Lord Jesus Christ saves

Let's be clear: nobody is saved from their sin just because they believe in God. As Jesus said, even the demons believe in God.[4] Further, nobody is saved by just believing in Jesus, because the question is what **specifically** do you believe about him? Salvation is only given to and received *"if you openly declare that Jesus is Lord and believe in your heart that God raised him from the dead"*.[5] Therefore a persuaded faith doesn't just believe "in God" or "in Jesus", but specifically believes that the Lord Jesus Christ died and then rose again three days later. The apostle Paul reminds us that this is **the central tenet** of our faith:

4 James 2:19
5 Romans 10:9

> *If Christ has not been raised, then your faith is useless and you are still guilty of your sins.*[6]

It follows that it is not an optional belief for a Christian, as without it *"you are still guilty of your sins"*.

Coming to persuasion about the resurrection

There's a fascinating account in the book of Acts of the apostle Paul preaching in Athens about Jesus being raised from the dead, and three ways in which the audience responded:

> *When they heard Paul speak about the resurrection of the dead, some laughed in contempt, but others said, "We want to hear more about this later." ...but some joined him and became believers.*[7]

Some mocked.
Others were not yet convinced.
Some became believers.

Which of these is your current response?

Further, how confident are you to answer someone who asks you, or more likely challenges you, about why you believe in the resurrection?

Because the resurrection is such a pivotal aspect of faith in Christ, it should be clear that every believer should have a very robust personal persuasion, as well as a clear apologetic — or reasoning — for why they believe it is true. Besides saying that "because the Bible says so", on what basis do you believe that Christ was raised from the dead? What convincing evidence can you present?

Evidence for the resurrection

I believe the resurrection is a crucial foundation in which every new believer must be established if they have any chance of remaining

6 1 Corinthians 15:17
7 Acts 17:32-34

firm in their faith. This is why we intentionally address it right at the start of the Follow Course, which aims to help people follow Jesus. We examine the claim of the resurrection, looking at viable evidence, sources and documentation that are virtually undisputed by historians—regardless of their personal faith or lack thereof. To make it memorable, we present the facts supporting the resurrection as "the four Es":

Fact 1: He EXISTED
Fact 2: His EXECUTION
Fact 3: The grave was EMPTY
Fact 4: The EARLY BELIEVERS

This is not the forum for a detailed explanation of this content, but since this is such an important part of having fully persuaded faith, here is a brief summary of these four facts to help you be persuaded:

Fact 1: He EXISTED. Jesus was not a mythical figure, but undisputedly a real person in history.

> *Jesus existed, and those vocal persons who deny it do so not because they have considered the evidence with the dispassionate eye of the historian, but because they have some other agenda that this denial serves.*[8]
>
> — **Bart Ehrman**, *secular agnostic professor and scholar*

Fact 2: His EXECUTION. Jesus did not just faint, but was dead. When his side was pierced by a spear, blood and water came out. We now know that the separation of serum and clotted blood in a person's body is conclusive medical evidence of a person's death.

Fact 3: The EMPTY tomb. If the tomb was not empty, the powerful enemies of Christianity—the Jewish Sanhedrin and the Romans—could have stopped the early church movement by

8 *Did Jesus Exist? The Historical Argument for Jesus of Nazareth* by Bart D. Ehrman

simply showing everyone that Jesus' tomb was still occupied, or displaying the dead body if found elsewhere.

Fact 4: The EARLY BELIEVERS. Many people saw the resurrected Christ. They touched him, heard his voice and saw him eat. At great personal risk the early believers publicly proclaimed that Jesus had risen from the dead, and people from all walks of life—and despite every predisposition to the contrary—came to believe in Jesus' resurrection. Even his brother James and his fiercest enemy Paul believed and proclaimed the resurrection.

Multitudes of men and women, both past and present, testify that the power of the risen Christ has transformed their lives. We know that Jesus is alive not only because of the historical and biblical evidence, but also because He has miraculously changed our lives.

Concluding the case for the resurrection

From all of the above, we conclude that believing in the resurrection of Jesus Christ is not blind faith. It is a confident faith based on the sure promises of God, the unique life he lived, and the overwhelming evidence that supports the resurrection.

Because the resurrection is true, miracles are possible. Because the resurrection is true, we can have a faith that does not fail, and nothing will separate us from his love. Because the resurrection is true, we are more than conquerors through him who loves us, Jesus Christ our Lord.

The greater your revelation of Jesus is as the resurrected Lord and Christ, the greater and stronger your faith will be. Your confidence in his Word will increase. His presence will be more real to you because you are persuaded that he is alive now. By the Holy Spirit you will experience his living Word guiding, encouraging and empowering you.

On the business of the King

I recall how in the week before arriving in London all those years ago, I had a significant fresh revelation of Jesus as "King". It came through a prophetic word that was given to us in the service when we were being sent out from Cape Town to start the church in London.

> *When you get to London, the enemy will say to you: "What are you doing here? Whose business are you on?" And you will reply: "We are on the business of the King!"*

What an encouragement that prophecy was, especially when we have felt intimidated, small and insignificant. I mean, who did we think we were, coming to this great city to "reach the nations"?

But this fresh revelation of the kingship of Jesus profoundly shaped the way I follow and serve him. Yes, while there would be opposition on the mission, we were not going to represent just any king, but the King of kings, the Lord of lords. He was for us, so who could be against us? I had a revelation that this was his business, not ours. We were his ambassadors, so he would take care of us — faithfully protecting, providing, supporting, and empowering us with all we needed to do all he had called us to. I understood that what I believed about God would determine how I represented him, and this revelation totally changed how I have been "*on the business of the King*".

I share this to show you what can happen and how empowering it is when you have a revelation of who the Lord Jesus Christ is. Sadly the converse is also true, when you fail to accurately recognise who he is, you limit what you will receive from him. We see this when Jesus arrived in his hometown Nazareth, and the people asked "*Isn't this the carpenter's son?*"[9] If that's all he is to you, then you may trust him to build you a table, or maybe a house. But imagine what he could do for and through you if you were persuaded that

9 Matthew 13:55 NIV

Jesus is the resurrected Christ the Lord, the King of all kings, whose business you are on as his ambassador. And friend, that is who he is, and that is who you are!

A faith that does not fail is established on being fully persuaded that Jesus is the resurrected Lord and Christ. I pray that you will be firmly established and immovable on this cornerstone truth.

PAUSE TO THINK AND TALK ABOUT IT

⇒ What is the one thing that you found most relevant or helpful in this chapter?

⇒ Consider and discuss how your understanding of who Christ is impacts the strength of your faith.

⇒ About the evidence for the resurrection, is there any one of the four facts presented that you struggle with? Why? Also consider what other evidence you may have to add to that mentioned.

⇒ What do you think about the point concerning us becoming familiar with using the name of Jesus? How could this be relevant to the way you pray or think?

CHAPTER THIRTEEN

To live is Christ

We exist to glorify God

- EVERY NATION LONDON CHURCH MISSION STATEMENT -

Facing his imminent death in a Roman prison, the apostle Paul summarised his life purpose with the phrase *"to live is Christ"*, or *"living means living for Christ"*.[1]

Looking at Paul's list in Romans chapter eight of all which cannot separate us from the love of God in Christ, I was intrigued to notice that he also includes *"life"* as one of the potential threats to our faith:

> *Neither death nor* ***life*** *... will ever be able to separate us from the love of God that is revealed in Christ Jesus our Lord.*

How can "life" separate me from God's love, and cause my faith to fail? The answer of course is that who and what we love and live for in this life will either draw us closer to God, or away from him. We are created as relational beings to love and to worship, so the question is not *will we love and worship*, but rather ***who*** *will we love and worship*? In this world there is a battle for the affections of our hearts, which is ultimately a battle for our faith.

Scripture is filled with warnings of how life *can* separate you from God's love, and is littered with accounts of those whose faith failed as their hearts were drawn away from their First Love. Take King Solomon. God had appeared to him twice, blessing him with

1 Philippians 1:21 NLT

wisdom, wealth and a long life, but Solomon's many wives turned his heart away from the Lord to worship other gods.[2] True love is always based on wholehearted devotion.

> *You must love the Lord your God with all your heart, all your soul, and all your mind.*[3]

The standard of love is always *"with ALL your heart"*.

No one ever stood at the wedding altar and vowed to love with *some* of my heart, or even with 99% of my heart! No, it's always with *ALL* of my heart, 100%.

Jesus rightly warned:

> *No one can serve two masters, since either he will hate one and love the other, or he will be devoted to one and despise the other.*[4]

Who and what we give our love and life to is the most important decision we will ever make.

The fight for your love

This fight for the deepest affections of our hearts has been a battleground from all the way back in the Garden, and no believer should underestimate this struggle. If Satan cannot cause your faith to fail through sin or circumstances, he will do all he can to try separating you through *tantalising offerings of life through the love of this world.* The apostle John warned believers:

> *Do not love this world nor the things it offers you, for when you love the world, you do not have the love of the Father in you.*[5]

He continues describing what the love of this world looks like:

2 1 Kings 11:3
3 Matthew 22:37
4 Matthew 6:24 CSB
5 1 John 2:15

a craving for physical pleasure (the lust of the flesh)
a craving for everything we see (the lust of the eyes)
pride in our achievements and possessions (the pride of life)[6]

I am sure that, like me, you can identify with these worldly longings of the heart which we are all susceptible to. However we must be clear that the love of this world is not only about our fleshly desires drawing us away from God. It is also very much about a spiritual battle of Christ vs antichrist, light vs darkness, spirit vs flesh, righteousness vs sin, truth vs lies, holiness vs wickedness, blessings vs curses, good vs evil, love vs hate, life vs death. It's a clash of kingdoms where Satan is the *"the thief (who) comes only to steal and kill and destroy"*, and Jesus who has *"come that they may have life, and have it to the full"*.[7]

This is the world into which Jesus came to give abundant and everlasting life through the gospel. It's in this world that we have been given free will to choose whom we will believe, serve and love, and there is much at stake in this choice.

Stay alert!

Even though we may be convinced of God's love today, we are all prone to temptations—some subtle and some very obvious—that seek to draw us away. We would do well to heed Peter's warning: *"Stay alert! Watch out for your great enemy, the devil. He prowls around like a roaring lion, looking for someone to devour."*[8]

Since I received the cancer diagnosis and while facing the possibility of an imminent end to this life, I have on a few occasions needed to honestly evaluate *why* I wanted to be healed and stay alive. What is my true motive? Is it for my pleasure or for God's purpose? Do I have FOMO—a fear of missing out of some pleasures in this life before I die? Squeezing in a few more snow-boarding adventures and memorable holiday trips? Or other desires of this world,

6 1 John 2:16 NLT and NIV
7 John 10:10 NIV
8 1 Peter 5:8

perhaps because I am not fully persuaded that *"to die is (really) gain"*?[9] Do I have any doubt about the spiritual reality of eternal life? Is his eternal presence truly the deepest longing of my heart?

I do know what I am persuaded about, but nevertheless in my struggling moments these questions have been subtle seeds of the world trying to pull my heart away from wholehearted devotion to my Lord. I also find that even very good things can easily become idols when they take prime place in my affections.

What has helped me at these times has been to come to God through King David's prayer, resulting in some very special *"times of refreshing"*[10] as my heart turned back to fully trusting God in this trouble I am facing:

> *Search me, God, and know my heart... Point out anything in me that offends you, and lead me along the path of everlasting life.*[11]

The blessing of repentance

What about you? Is there any love of this world drawing you away right now? Perhaps it's been a subtle drift of your heart away from choosing God's love and life. Or like the prodigal son, your choices and rebellion have led you to the proverbial pigsty of this world, and you have now come to your senses with your heart yearning, *"I will go home to my father."*[12]

If that's where you are at, then please know that the Father is waiting and longing for you to come back to him through Jesus, who is the Way. The return home starts with repentance, which includes *a turning from and a turning to*, a change of heart and mind towards both God and sin. True repentance starts with a revelation of the goodness of God;[13] followed by recognising the utter depravity of sin and the empty deception of the love of this

9 Philippians 1:21
10 Acts 3:19
11 Psalm 139:23-24
12 Luke 15:18
13 Romans 2:4 NKJV

world; then turning in surrender and faith to receive forgiveness and restoration in God's presence:

> *Now repent of your sins and turn to God, so that your sins may be wiped away. Then times of refreshment will come from the presence of the Lord.*[14]

Living in God's presence

You were made to live fully loved in his holy presence. Yes, God is *omnipresent*, meaning he is everywhere at all times, and there is nowhere to flee from him. But his *holy presence* is where you experience his reality with you, where the so-called veil has been removed[15] and you know him and hear his voice. This is his holy presence where there is fullness of joy. This is how we are created to live with God in this world.

The question is: are you persuaded that living fully loved in God's presence is what you were made for? The more your eyes open to these spiritual realities, the more persuaded you will be to choose life through Jesus, and reject what the deceptive love of this world offers.

Choose life today

I encourage you to slow down a little right now and hear God speak to you through these words of Moses, and consider your response:

> *Today I have given you the choice between life and death, between blessings and curses. Now I call on heaven and earth to witness the choice you make.* ***Oh, that you would choose life,*** *so that you and your descendants might live! You can make this choice by loving the Lord your God, obeying him, and committing yourself firmly to him. This is the key to your life.*[16]

14 Acts 3:19-20
15 2 Corinthians 3:12-18
16 Deuteronomy 30:19-20

Friend, you choose true life when you choose God's love.

This world and its ways can never satisfy the true longings of your heart. Only by wholehearted devotion to Jesus, who presented himself as the Way, the Truth and *the Life,*[17] can we find the life in all its fullness we are all searching for.

Living on purpose in this world, but not of it

Jesus commissioned his followers to *go into all the world,* yet was also deeply concerned about how they would live in this world without being consumed by it. His prayer to the Father for his disciples is revealing:

> *I'm not asking you to take them out of the world, but to keep them safe from the evil one.*[18]

Reading this verse in isolation would miss the point of Jesus' prayer. This is not a plea to just to keep the disciples "safe and surviving" against the temptations of the world and wickedness of Satan. Jesus completes this prayer with a commissioning of the disciples to go into the world just as he himself was sent into the world:

> *Just as you sent me into the world, I am sending them into the world.*[19]

Living sent by Jesus

This "sending" here is the Greek word "apostellō", meaning *"a personal commissioning, sent on a defined mission by a superior".*[20] Jesus is praying that every disciple will fulfil their appointed assignment in this life.

17 John 14:6
18 John 17:15
19 John 17:18
20 Strong's NT 649

For I know the plans I have for you...[21]
I have called you by name, and you are mine...[22]
Come, follow me, and I will make you...[23]
Therefore go and make disciples of all the nations...[24]

A persuasion that God has a unique call and purpose for your life will greatly affect the way you live this life. When the apostle Paul considered the trouble and trials he went through, it was his sense of purpose which gave him the perspective he needed to endure and make sense of it all:

> *And I want you to know, my dear brothers and sisters, that everything that has happened to me here has helped to spread the Good News.*[25]

Here Paul states that his mission is "*to spread the Good News*". This is the mission every disciple is personally sent on by our Superior, the resurrected Jesus Christ the Lord. He has been given all authority in heaven and on earth, and now sends—*apostellō*—all disciples to be his witnesses from wherever we are all the way to the ends of the earth, *going and making disciples of all nations.*

This is not just a sending away into the world in your own strength, but like Jesus promised, "*I am with you always, even to the end of the age.*"[26]

Just as Jesus incarnate always experienced the presence of the Father and the Holy Spirit as he fulfilled his purpose, so too every disciple on mission can know the presence and power of God as we go into all the world. We are not just sent away into the world, but rather *we go with him as we go for him.* Practising his presence

21 Jeremiah 29:11
22 Isaiah 43:1
23 Matthew 4:19
24 Matthew 28:19
25 Philippians 1:12
26 Matthew 28:20

is a precious and empowering habit to cultivate as you pursue his purpose.

To live is Christ

Earlier I asked the question: *if we are persuaded by these things, how then will we live this life?* Or, *how do these certainties we claim to believe affect the way we live, especially in times of trouble?*

It's important to remember that when the apostle Paul stated his life purpose as *"living means living for Christ"*, he was under great pressure facing the real prospect of death in a Roman jail. This was a time when Paul's faith could so easily have failed, but rather we see that he holds fast to his persuasions and purpose even in the face of death.

> *For me,* ***living means living for Christ****, and dying is even better. But if I live, I can do more fruitful work for Christ. So I really don't know which is better. I'm torn between two desires: I long to go and be with Christ, which would be far better for me. But for your sakes, it is better that I continue to live.*[27]

Paul connects living for Christ with his life purpose. As much as he longs to be eternally with Christ, he is torn between what is better for him, and what is better for the disciples. He concludes that *for their sake it is better that he continues to live*. Imagine that, choosing to stay on earth with all its troubles, for the sake of others! This is the power of purpose, drawing one to live at the expense of self for the benefit of others, just as Jesus did.

Choosing to live

In my own way I can identify with Paul as my life hangs in the balance under the threat of cancer. Reading this passage, I noticed that Paul said: *"I really don't know which I should choose."* In response I asked the Lord: *"Did Paul have a choice to live or die? Do I have a choice, Lord?"*

27 Philippians 1:21-24

All I can say is that I sensed a green light in my spirit to ask the Lord that I would continue to live. Not for any pleasure or love for this world. I genuinely have no desire for that. But I have what I can only describe as a great sense of purpose still to fulfil, and I am asking the Lord to make that possible by keeping me alive for as long as it takes to say, "I finished the work you assigned me to do."

There is more

At our Every Nation London Church thirty-year anniversary last year, the prophetic sense we had was that "there is more", from when the Lord said to Joshua: *"You've had a good, long life, but there is a lot of land still to be taken."*[28]

For me this includes our GOEurope2040 vision, which is that by God's grace we will plant a campus-reaching church in every European nation by 2040. I so want to serve to see that fulfilled! And there are books and resources that I feel called to write, wisdom to pass on, and leaders to raise and come alongside for this mission with these resources. On most days I wake up thankful that I get another day to live for Christ by doing this.

In the light of this, I remain persuaded that cancer will not determine my death or legacy. Only my Lord will, when his work for me is done. Until then, I choose life, which is to live for Christ's great purpose in our generation.

Commit to God's calling

Take a moment to consider how you feel about your divine calling and purpose. Are you living for something greater than yourself? Can you confidently say, *"I am living for Christ,"* meaning that his mission is significantly determining your priorities, choices and the way you are living? Or have you been drawn by the desires and lust of this world into a self-centred what's-in-it-for-me life?

Living for self or this world is *not* the way to experience abundant life. It's only in laying down our lives that we find them.

28 Joshua 13:1 The Message

> *If you cling to your life, you will lose it; but if you give up your life for me, you will find it.*[29]

Friend, as you consider who and what you are living for, and if you are ready now, I urge you to surrender to living wholeheartedly for Christ now by boldly declaring:

> *My Lord Jesus Christ, I choose your life by choosing to live wholeheartedly with you and for you!*

I pray that as you do that now, you will receive a fresh empowering by God the Holy Spirit, filling your heart with his presence, and receiving a renewed sense of purpose stirring your heart with clarity of how and where he is calling you to serve him for his mission.

Living to glorify God

"*Living to glorify God*" is another way to summarise a believer's life purpose. I believe that you can't go wrong in any area of your life if you make this your simple goal.

To "glorify God" is to first personally recognise God for who he truly is in his greatness and goodness, and in response, to live in a way that honours and reveals him as such to the world.

Jesus is our perfect example of living for the Father's glory. As he "*became flesh*", we saw his glory through the way he "*made his dwelling among us*".[30] In the same way, as his image bearers and ambassadors, we glorify him by living in every way that those around us will know and experience God as he truly is. We glorify God when we love like Jesus, forgive like Jesus, serve like Jesus, minister like Jesus, humble ourselves like Jesus.

> *God is revealed to the world as we intentionally live to glorify him.*

29 Matthew 10:39
30 John 1:14 NIV

We exist to glorify God

Many years ago, as we were wrestling to articulate our Every Nation London church's mission statement, we concluded that it would start with: "*We exist to glorify God...*" This one statement helps us to both decide or evaluate our actions, choices, and priorities with just one simple question: does this (or did this) bring glory to God?

When the apostle Paul was helping the believers in Corinth navigate some difficult theological and practical issues in the church, he lifted their eyes up above these debates and set a very simple goal for them:

> *So whether you eat or drink, or whatever you do, do it all for the glory of God.*[31]
>
> *So whether we are here in this body or away from this body, our goal is to please him.*[32]

Do it all to the glory of God.

Even eating and drinking.

In everything, make it your goal to please him.

What would it look like if you and I — and all believers around the world — lived with that simple but profound goal in mind every day?

31 1 Corinthians 10:31

32 2 Corinthians 5:9

PAUSE TO THINK AND TALK ABOUT IT

⇒ What is the one thing that you found most relevant or helpful in this chapter?

⇒ Remembering Romans 8:38, are there any things in "life" — even good things — that have the potential to separate you from God's love? How can you stay alert to make sure they don't?

⇒ Is God's eternal presence truly the deepest longing of your heart? Or have worldly longings for pleasure, things or achievements drawn you away?

⇒ Can you write down what you believe your calling from God is?

⇒ Consider the words of Moses: do you choose life or death? Will you choose life by living intentionally and wholeheartedly to glorify God?

CHAPTER FOURTEEN

To die is gain

Then we will be with the Lord forever[1]

- THE APOSTLE PAUL -

It has now been two months since I started writing this book. I am still under "best end of life care" and the medical prognosis points to the brutal reality that my death by cancer is imminent. I am no longer having any scans, so I have no idea what the forty plus tumours are doing in my brain, nor what is happening with those that were growing in my spine, back and other places.

That said, I am still feeling very well, Ali says I am still looking well(!). We continue to face these brutal cancer facts by faith, still fully convinced in God's promises for my healing and that I will live out his purposes for my life.

But frankly, I may also have died by the time you read this.

If that is the case, I want you to know that neither death nor cancer has had any victory. My faith has not failed in this battle against cancer, because my faith is not built on the mystery of healing, but on the certainty of the gift of eternal life, the unchanging love of God, and the resurrected Lord Jesus Christ. These faith persuasions are the unshakable rock solid foundations on which I have lived, and by which I am convinced that nothing—even death—can indeed separate me from the love of God that is in Christ Jesus my Lord.

1 1 Thessalonians 4:17

Considering death

One thing about a terminal cancer diagnosis is that you get some time to think about dying. Once I got past the initial range of emotional and practical responses, I took quite a bit of time to consider the reality of death that was now staring me square in the face. What do I really believe about death and eternity? How do I *feel* about it? Am I in any way afraid of dying, and if so, why? Am I convinced that *"to die is gain"?*

Do I, like the Welsh poet Dylan Thomas wrote, *"Rage, rage against the dying of the light,"*[2] resisting the inevitable, or am I at peace to enter what awaits me after my final earthly breath?

What happens when we die?

When the actor Keanu Reeves was asked this question on a late night show, he answered: *"I know that the ones who love us will miss us."* I think that's a pretty wise and thoughtful response worth all of us considering as part of facing death. It's never just about us, but also very much about the ones we leave behind. In my situation, I feel this acutely for my precious natural and spiritual family. One strong feeling I have had to confront is that I am somehow *abandoning* my Ali and my precious daughters, who have so much life still before them. As I brought this burden to the Lord, I sensed the Spirit saying: *"Wolfi, you can trust me with them."* It definitely isn't easy, but this word has given me a wonderful comfort and peace ever since.

So what does happen when we die?

Of course, what we usually mean with this question is *what happens to a person when they die?* Or to *us* when we die?

It's one of the big questions of life. Most of us probably have some kind of philosophical or theological answers or ideas about what happens after death, and when and how Jesus returns on the Last Day.

2 Poem *Do not go gentle into that good night* by Dylan Thomas (1914-1953)

When the apostle Paul contemplated his choice between living and dying, he concluded, *"I'm torn between two desires: I long to go and be with Christ, which would be far better for me."*[3] Here he uses the word *"long"* (Greek: epithumia[4]) to express his anticipation of going to be with Christ. I understand this word to mean *"a passionate longing built on strong feelings inspired by faith"*. Read that again and see that he is not just communicating the *facts he believes* about death, but *how he feels* about it.

Paul passionately longs to be with the Lord forever, and his strong feelings are grounded in his persuaded faith about eternity, the resurrection, and that physical death was not the end of life for the believer but a glorious transition into the gift of eternal life through the gospel of the Lord Jesus Christ.

Do I *long* to be with my Lord forever?

As I faced the possibility of my own imminent death, I have come to realise that there is a big difference between saying I believe some *facts* about eternity and my longing or *feelings* about eternity. It's easy to quote a few Bible verses on the topic, but quite another to pause and ponder the reality of my theology on the subject. Like this one:

> *Yes, we are fully confident, and we would rather be away from these earthly bodies, for then we will be at home with the Lord.*[5]

I believe this verse to mean that when I die, I will immediately be *in heaven in the presence of Jesus*! Can you imagine that! In one moment I will be in eternity. Yes there may be questions about how and when exactly the body is resurrected with my soul, but the promise remains: I will be in the presence of my Saviour and Lord! I will see his glory face to face! We may not know exactly what it will be like, but we long for eternity because we are eternal beings.

3 Philippians 1:23
4 Strong's NT 1939
5 2 Corinthians 5:8

God has made everything beautiful for its own time. He has planted eternity in the human heart.[6]

Scripture describes the entrance to eternity like this:

And I heard a loud voice from the throne saying, "Look! God's dwelling place is now among the people, and he will dwell with them. They will be his people, and God himself will be with them and be their God. He will wipe every tear from their eyes. There will be no more death or mourning or crying or pain, for the old order of things has passed away."[7]

All suffering will be gone. Every tear wiped away. No more fear, tears, pain, and even death. No cancer! There will be perfect justice. Eternal joy, peace, and fulfilment. What an incredible hope!

I can only imagine

The *feelings* of what it will be like to enter heaven and come face to face with the Saviour are captured well in the popular Christian song *I can only imagine* by the band MercyMe, in which the lead singer Bart Millard imagines what it would be like for his deceased father to meet God in heaven:

I can only imagine
What it will be like
When I walk by your side
I can only imagine
What my eyes would see
When your face is before me
I can only imagine
Surrounded by your glory
What will my heart feel?
Will I dance for you Jesus
Or in awe of you be still?

6 Ecclesiastes 3:11
7 Revelation 21:3-4 NIV

Will I stand in your presence
Or to my knees, will I fall?
Will I sing hallelujah?
Will I be able to speak at all?
I can only imagine

Glimpses of glory

Can you imagine what heaven is like? Being face to face with God? Consider the most intimate moments you have ever had with the Father, Son or Holy Spirit. Perhaps as he revealed himself to you through his Word. Or as you worshipped him with reckless abandon. Or as you felt the weight of guilt and shame miraculously lift off you as his amazing grace washed your sin away. Or as you felt his heartbeat for that homeless man you stopped to acknowledge and bless in his name. Or what you felt as you fellowshipped in true unity with his body the church. Imagine experiencing that perpetually—never ending and never changing. David the Psalmist expressed it like this:

> *In your presence is fullness of joy, in your right hand there are pleasures forevermore.*[8]

Imagine uncontainable ecstatic enraptured *joy!*

Imagine pure unadulterated glorious holy *pleasure!*

In this life we get to *taste and see that the Lord is good,*[9] but as much as we do, it's only a glimpse of glory. We can only imagine encountering his holy perfection face to face, but we are persuaded this will be the reality for every believer for eternity. Wow!

The eternal prize that awaits

In his final letter to Timothy, the apostle Paul wrote a kind of personal obituary as he contemplates the end of his earthly life, summing it up like this:

8 Psalm 16:11b Amplified Bible, Classic Edition
9 Psalm 34:8

> *I have fought the good fight, I have finished the race, and I have remained faithful. And now the prize awaits me—the crown of righteousness, which the Lord, the righteous Judge, will give me on the day of his return. And the prize is not just for me but for all who eagerly look forward to his appearing.*[10]

What a way to finish!

His faith has not failed.

Nothing has separated him from the love of God in Christ Jesus.

Now it's time for him to receive the crown, the one prize he has lived for and longed for since meeting Jesus on the road to Damascus.

The prize is not just for Paul, but for all the multitude *who eagerly look forward to Jesus' appearing,* like the apostle John records seeing in this vision:

> *After this I looked, and there before me was a great multitude that no one could count, from every nation, tribe, people and language, standing before the throne and before the Lamb. They were wearing white robes and were holding palm branches in their hands. And they cried out in a loud voice: "Salvation belongs to our God, who sits on the throne, and to the Lamb."*[11]

Friend, beyond all the prayers for my healing and to fulfil my remaining purpose in this life, my greater prayer is that your faith would not fail, and that we will be together with the Lord forever.

> *Now all glory to God, who is able to keep you from falling away and will bring you with great joy into his glorious presence without a single fault.*[12]

---

10 2 Timothy 4:7-8

11 Revelation 7:9-10 NIV

12 Jude 1:24

PAUSE TO THINK AND TALK ABOUT IT

⇒ What is the one thing that you found most relevant or helpful in this chapter?

⇒ What is your reaction to the descriptions of eternal life in this chapter? What does your reaction reveal about your perception of God's character?

⇒ Read Paul's obituary in 2 Timothy 4 again. Through these verses I'm always challenged to consider how I would sum up my life in a few sentences. Perhaps that is an exercise for all of us to do?

TOOLKIT

How to grow your faith through REAPing the Bible

I am assuming that we have been reminded of the importance of the Bible as the foundation of all faith, and that without an understanding of and rich engagement with the scriptures, we will not be able to have a strong flourishing faith.

In this practical toolkit, I will share tips on how you can grow in richly engaging with God daily through the Bible and prayer. This is by far the most important spiritual discipline for every follower of Jesus to develop. It is also very much a spiritual desire: we do this because our spirit craves the delight of rich intimacy with God through his Word and Spirit.

You cannot separate your regular daily spiritual practice of meaningful engagement with God from Jesus' invitation to abide (remain) in him and his words, and the promise of resulting intimacy and spiritual fruitfulness, answered prayer, and great glory brought to your Father.

> *But if you remain in me and my words remain in you, you may ask for anything you want, and it will be granted! When you produce much fruit, you are my true disciples. This brings great glory to my Father.*[1]

But how do we REAP the Word?

In what we call discipleship or helping others to follow Jesus, I want to be cautious that we do not just instruct people *what to do*, but also very much help them with *how to do* it. For example, do I say *you must* read your Bible, or do I also teach *how you can read* the Bible?

Many years ago at Every Nation London, it dawned on me that we desperately needed to do something to change our Bible reading and prayer culture by introducing a common, transferable, memorable and biblical approach to this crucial spiritual practice. I was convinced that this one change would make a significant difference to the way we would experience God through scripture. It has indeed been the case for me personally and also for our Bible and prayer engagement culture across the church community.

Here's the REAPing pattern we use

Don't just read the Bible—REAP it! REAP is a verb that sets out a practical approach to help you meaningfully engage with God through the Bible. The process is:

R for **Read** the Word
E for **Examine** the Word
A for **Apply** the Word
P for **Pray** the Word

1 John 15:7-8

Read the Word

Choose a book in the Bible to start reading. Don't just read randomly, but systematically, because "systematic reading results in specific leading", as we like to say.

Read a short portion of scripture every day, then continue on the next day from where you ended. Don't be discouraged if you miss a day. Simply start again where you had last stopped.

For example, try reading slowly through the book of Mark, only 5 to 10 verses a day, or even less. It is a great way to get to know Jesus and his teaching.

Examine the Word

Ask: who is it written to? Why? What is it about? What was the context in time and place? What do I learn from this?

Apply the Word

Consider how this passage relates to your life now. Then ask: what does this teach about God? What truth stands out to me? How is my faith strengthened from this passage? What does this passage call me to believe, and how do I obey the truth in this text?

Pray the Word

Talk to God about what you have read. Ask Him for wisdom to help you understand, and for strength and courage to obey this truth.

Use these truths you have read to pray for yourself, your loved ones, the church, people who don't yet know Jesus, and the world.

Expand your prayer using the ACTS outline:

A = **Acknowledge** and **Adoration** for who He is.
C = **Confess** your faith in Christ, and bring any sin to Him.
T = **Thank** God for your salvation and all He has done.
S = **Supplication**, bringing your needs, requests and intercession (prayer for others) to the Father in the name of Jesus Christ.

Pray for the three Ns: **Needs, Neighbours** and **Nations**. This helps me to broaden what I bring to God in prayer: the list of needs all around me, but also my neighbours who do not yet know the gospel, and then the nations—world-changing prayers asking for the nations as our inheritance, and God's intervention in the issues affecting people across the earth.

We can ask ourselves: if God answered all my prayers I prayed last week, what kind of world would we be living in? Faith grows as we pray big prayers in faith.

Use a journal

Listen to God's voice by using a daily journal to record what you are hearing.

I have a habit of using a page-a-day journal in which I write down my responses under the REAP headings. Even if you just write down a verse you read, and one thought each day, coming with a pen shows that you expect to receive something that will be worth remembering.

Culture is also established by having an expectation to receive. For example, we ask each other: "Where are you REAPING in the Bible at the moment, and what is God saying to you through his Word?"

Faith grows as we come to Jesus through his Word and through prayer.

Acknowledging that we have never been alone in this battle

There are very few, if any, battles in life that one should fight alone. The fight for our faith is definitely not one of them. It is in these times that we discover who our true faith friends and spiritual family are.

It is devastating to hear the words, "You have cancer." Ali and I cannot overstate how grateful we are for the many faith-filled followers of Jesus from around the world who have carried us with unwavering faith in response to this testing trial.

We do not know why some are healed, and some are not. However this has caused us to stop relying on ourselves and our own understanding, learning to trust only in the God who raises the dead.

We have been strengthened through the prayers of many, and by the extraordinary lengths our spiritual family will go to to express that they are there for one another. A special mention that comes to mind is for Pastors Cathy and Jim Laffoon, whom we are sure prayed for us every single day, together with Pastor Brett Fuller who was a champion encourager all along the way. Pastor Russ Austin travelled over from Florida to London to be with me for just one short but such an encouraging weekend in Wales, reminding that fledgling church plant that we do not despise the days of small beginnings. Thank you Russ!

Soon after the initial diagnosis, one of our dear friends and London church elders, Liz Lugt, initiated a weekly prayer meeting, with the single purpose of seeking God's Word and will for my healing and life. That meeting has continued uninterrupted since. Together with Ali, these relentless prayer warriors included Adesola Atanda, Liz Henderson, Christilene Kiewiets, Audette Levy, Mike Levy and Hirondina Pestana.

To the staff from Every Nation global offices, and to many, many others who know who you are, thank you!

WOLFI ECKLEBEN
July 2024

About the author

Wolfgang, or as he was affectionately known, Wolfi, was passionate about helping people to live well, love well, and lead well. He was married to Ali, together with whom he founded the Every Nation Church London in 1993. Wolfi also fulfilled a strategic leadership role among Every Nation churches in Europe and globally. He and Ali have two daughters.

Born in Namibia with German as his home language, he grew up in South Africa. He was not raised in a Christian home, but became a Christ follower in his late teens. After university and working as a project manager for a large construction company, his life took a new trajectory as he answered a call to vocational ministry. This led him and Ali to hear God's call to start a new church in London, and in 1993, having never been there before, and knowing no one, they landed at Heathrow Airport with their "two backpacks and a vision", as Wolfi would later put it.

It has been an incredible God-adventure touching countless lives and nations through church planting, campus ministry and a passion to see the good news of God's amazing grace experienced by every person, and God's Kingdom come in every sphere of society.

Back in his youth, he once ran a sub four-minute mile and had completed a couple of London marathons, but later Wolfi preferred "board" meetings — especially the snowboard and stand up paddle-board type.

Further resources

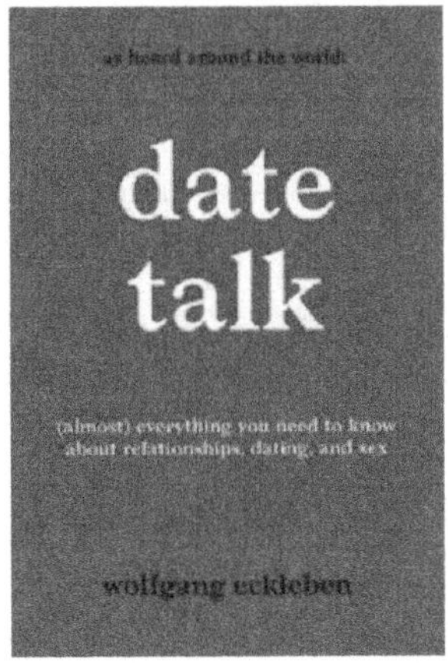

Books

Available on Amazon, various retailers and Every Nation Churches (proceeds to Every Nation Campus ministries):

- *The Art of Loving Well* covers ten powerful ways to change your relational climate.
- *DateTalk,* a book for not-yet-marrieds which looks at *"(almost) everything you need to know about dating, relationships and sex"*.

Course

- "The Follow Course", an intentional three-part journey to help you grow as a follower of Jesus. Available to church leaders from Every Nation London.

Online

- Facebook page: *The Art of Loving Well*
- Church Website: *www.everynation.london*
- Blog: *www.wolfinlondon.com*
- On YouTube: watch the *DateTalk* series for free via 6x28 minute videos, plus many other teachings.

God is able to keep you

Now all glory to God, who is able to keep you from falling away and will bring you with great joy into his glorious presence without a single fault.

JUDE 1:24

Printed in Great Britain
by Amazon

59909912R00080